THE IMPRISONMENT
OF THE INNOCENT

This book is dedicated to the memories of all those innocent people who have spent various periods of time in prison for offences which they had not committed and to the few who in the past had paid the ultimate price

THE
IMPRISONMENT
OF THE
INNOCENT

Malcolm Sinclair

B.A. (Law), LL.B (Hons.) Barrister

Frederick Muller Limited
London

First published in Great Britain in 1983
by Frederick Muller Limited,
Dataday House, Alexandra Road, London SW19 7JZ

British Library Cataloguing in Publication Data

Sinclair, Malcolm.
    Imprisonment of the innocent.
    1. Bail—England
    I. Title
    344.205'72   KD8340

ISBN 0–584–50007–6

Phototypeset by Input Typesetting Ltd.
Printed in Great Britain by Billing & Sons Ltd., Worcester

PREFACE

For those who have picked this book up expecting a concerted attack on the police force or the proliferation of extreme left or right wing views of one political doctrine or another, my advice is simply to replace the book immediately, for they may be gravely disappointed.

The aim of this book is threefold:

First and perhaps easiest, to destroy the myth that only those people who are guilty of criminal offences serve periods of imprisonment.

Second and perhaps most difficult, to illustrate how our legal system not only allows this to occur but also appears in many ways, albeit unintentionally, to strive towards this particular aim.

Third is the hope that the reader who is ever unfortunate enough to find himself caught up within our legal system will adopt a cautious approach as a result of reading this book, instead of a blind faith which regrettably has little factual foundation.

This book is not intended for the lawyer who wishes to get involved in highly complex legal arguments which few people other than lawyers could understand, let alone agree with. Nor is it for politicians who wish to use it in order to discredit the political beliefs of opponents or to generate criticism for the justification of their own political beliefs. It is meant for ordinary people, and by that I mean people who work in order to provide a living for themselves or their families; who pay mortgages or rent in order to keep a roof over their heads; who endeavour to bring up their children in a responsible manner and who from their experience know many of the realities of life yet instinctively believe in our system as the eventual protection against injustice.

This book, with the exception of certain minor but necessary deviations, is concerned only with the criminal law, and the general method adopted in order to achieve the book's aims is by highlighting the differences between the theory and the practice of this branch of the law. By the theory I mean that which the ordinary person believes in, by practice I mean that which actually occurs.

Having established the aims of the book and its intended audience the final problem concerned the method to be adopted in writing it. As it was not going to be written for lawyers the normal method of writing for lawyers could be avoided. However, as the book was to be about fact as opposed to fiction, many of the methods utilised when writing fiction had also to be discarded.

I came to the conclusion that a suitable method would be, during the first half of the book, to state the facts as they actually occur, as simply as I was able but without losing the essential ingredient of truth. These facts are coupled, where necessary, with observation, comment and inferences which can readily and reasonably be drawn from the facts. Often, in order to achieve lucidity for the reader, it is necessary to generalise, but in so doing every endeavour is made not in any way to distort reality or to sacrifice truth upon the altar of drama.

The second half of the book is mainly devoted to actual case histories which I trust will clearly illustrate many of the points which have been made in the first half. The aim in adopting the method chosen has been that by the end of the book the reader will have a clearer picture of the reality of the situation within the criminal law branch of the legal system, which regularly and tragically leads to the imprisonment of the innocent. Whether I achieve this aim is a question which only you, the reader, will be able to answer.

THE POLICE

The theory that a police officer is an officer of the law whose job is to enforce the law, bring the guilty to justice, remain staunchly aloof and independent in the collection of evidence, and present such evidence in an honest, unbiased and accurate manner, is a theory which fails to assert itself in practice.

Of course there are police officers who make every effort to comply with the image required of them, but to many ambition and the will to progress within their careers, coupled with prejudices of one sort or another, soon take over whenever a conflict arises between doing the right thing and advancing their careers.

Undoubtedly one of the primary qualifications for advancement within the force is the successful collection of evidence in order to obtain convictions, for it would be preposterous to assume that a police officer could advance to the higher ranks if the number of convictions which he managed to be directly or indirectly responsible for was small.

If one accepts the part which the ability to obtain convictions plays in the advancement of the policeman's career, one may begin to appreciate the many dangers which threaten the individual from the beginning of the investigative process to the eventual trial.

Before an individual can be convicted of any criminal offence he has either to plead guilty to the offence or to be found guilty of it. A prerequisite of such a determination is that in the majority of cases the person will have been arrested. The arrest will normally be made by an investigating police officer, who will often give evidence at the trial if the person pleads not guilty.

In theory a police officer has the power to arrest without a

1

warrant anyone whom he with reasonable cause suspects has committed any one of a number of offences from the theft of a reel of cotton to murder. There is a small number of offences for which the police officer will require a warrant in order to make an arrest. These types of offences are deemed to be comparatively trivial, and the police officer can obtain such a warrant by providing information to a Magistrate, whereupon its issue will often be a mere formality. However, in the majority of cases the police officer has the power to arrest without a warrant, and it is with these cases that we are mainly concerned.

The phrase 'reasonable cause' demands close examination, for in most other branches of the law the word reasonable imports an objective test. That is to say that the reasonable man viewing the situation from a distance with knowledge of the facts would say that the police officer was right in making the arrest in question. However, in the criminal law the phrase tends to be given a much wider definition, importing much more of a subjective test, namely whether a reasonable police officer would consider it right to make an arrest in the circumstances. Alternatively the word reasonable becomes attached to the word suspicion, so that the phrase 'whom he with reasonable cause suspects', becomes 'whom he reasonably suspects'.

The dangers of such a wide subjective interpretation will soon become apparent to the reader, especially if he bears in mind that there can be few 'reasonable men' who could accept that a citizen can be lawfully arrested without the police officer having at the time of the arrest some evidence, however little, to put before a court. Yet the practice is such that this very situation easily can and does occur.

Thus, for example, a police officer may have information that a person may have property illegally in his possession. He goes to the person's home, finds the property, and in such circumstances an arrest will normally follow. Or a police officer may take a statement from a potential witness which contains evidence implicating another person in a criminal offence. The police officer will interview the person implicated and even if he denies any involvement an arrest may still follow. In both examples it would be difficult to justify that an arrest ought not to be made, for at the time of the arrest the

2

police officer will have some evidence to put before a court. However, a typical situation is one in which a police officer, having already arrested a person who may have committed a serious offence, is informed by the person he has arrested that another man committed the offence with him. It is a cardinal rule of evidence, with very few exceptions, that what one person says in a written statement implicating another person is not evidence against that other person. Further, this situation differs from the earlier examples because if the 'other man' is to be arrested he will stand trial as a co-accused with the man who, simply put, 'has dropped him in it', and, as the police officer well knows when he goes to interview the other man, one co-accused cannot be forced to give evidence against another at their trial. The police officer goes to the other man's home to interview him, whereupon the other man denies all involvement in the alleged offence. It also transpires that there could be many reasons why the person arrested made the allegations, none of which has anything to do with the offence he was arrested for. Notwithstanding the denial and notwithstanding that at that stage the police officer does not have a shred of evidence to put before a court, the man will in many cases be arrested and taken into custody. However, having arrested the person, the police officer will not have formally charged him with the offence and he knows that if he doesn't come up with some evidence soon the man will have to be released. It is in this type of situation that some of the greatest threats to liberty lie.

Once the police officer has arrested the citizen, without a shred of admissible evidence against him, the fact that he may be totally innocent of the alleged offence fades into comparative insignificance. The investigating police officer suffers little or no damage of any description whatever the eventual outcome. If the man is later charged he will subsequently stand his trial; if he is not charged he will be released. But the man arrested may immediately suffer enormous damage. Assume that, as in so many cases, the man is not in fact charged, or is charged and later acquitted. If he has been arrested at his home and he is a family man with children, anxiety, often coupled with a sense of shame, will immediately afflict his wife and family. Their friends, acquaintances and neighbours will soon become aware of the situation and, apart from perhaps a few closest friends, the family may find themselves virtually ostracized from the community within which they have tried to develop their lives. Word travels fast, and the man's children will in many cases find themselves being tormented by other children at school. If the man is arrested at work his working relationship with his workmates may never be quite the same. Even if released without being charged, or if eventually acquitted at his trial, suspicion will remain among those who have heard about the arrest.

It is necessary for me to make it quite clear to the reader at this stage that whether the man is imprisoned and then released without being charged, or whether he is charged and later acquitted, neither he nor his family have any right to compensation for the hardship they will have suffered unless he can successfully sue in a civil court for wrongful arrest/false imprisonment, and because of the wide powers of arrest given to police officers and the even wider interpretation put on those powers by the courts, only in the most blatant cases is he likely to succeed. Further, to sue in civil proceedings requires money, unless legal aid is granted, and is a very lengthy process which even if successful could result in him having to pay a substantial amount towards his legal costs. It follows, therefore, that for all practical purposes the innocent man who has spent time in prison has no real redress against those responsible for allowing the situation to occur in the first place. The relevance of this is that when he makes his arrest the experienced police officer knows that there is virtually no possibility of the person whom he has arrested taking any action against him.

Having arrested the citizen, the police officer will then usually take him to a police station, where he will be imprisoned in a cell. If the police officer hasn't already formally charged him, he will subsequently interview him. The states of mind of the police officer and the suspect bear interesting comparison immediately prior to the interview. The state of mind of the citizen who has been arrested will often vary depending upon whether or not he has had previous dealings with the police. The citizen who has never had any real dealings with the police and who has never been in trouble before is often the most vulnerable at this stage, for assuming he is innocent of the alleged offence he cannot fully understand what is happening. To him it is some sort of ghastly mistake, and he will still treat the police officer more as a friend than as an enemy. The police officer, on the other hand, will be viewing the individual purely as a suspect and as a possible future conviction. If the officer has also made the arrest without any admissible evidence he will be looking for some evidence against the suspect before formally charging him, for otherwise the suspect will have to be released. His primary concern, therefore, is not necessarily whether the individual concerned is in fact guilty of the alleged offence but whether the result of the interview will assist in securing a conviction. With such an approach a certain degree of bias is inherent.

In theory the citizen should at this stage be allowed the services of a solicitor, for there is a rule which states that every person at any stage of an investigation should be able to communicate and consult privately with a solicitor. This is so even if he is in custody, provided that in such a case no unreasonable delay or hindrance is caused to the processes of investigation or the administration of justice.

In practice, however, if the officer has arrested someone without any evidence which would be admissible in a court, or if he believes the evidence he has may be insufficient to obtain a conviction, the last person the officer will want to see is a solicitor advising his client about his legal rights. He will therefore often justify delaying the solicitor from seeing the suspect on the grounds that hindrance would be caused to his investigation. Further, such delaying tactics will often continue until the suspect is eventually formally charged. Again it is necessary to emphasise that the question whether the officer's tactics in preventing the solicitor from seeing his client are justified or not will rarely be decided. It follows, therefore, that in the situations when such tactics are wholly unjustified the citizen has no effective remedy.

In any event it is plain to see that a rule designed to protect the citizen while he is in police custody is a rule without teeth, and the reality of the situation is that a citizen in police custody has no right whatsoever to see a solicitor at this most important stage of the investigative process if the senior investigating police officer doesn't want him to. Thus the citizen is alone in police custody.

The interview, or perhaps interrogation is a better word to describe the form which the interview will take, will nearly always be one where the senior officer in charge of the case and at least one other officer who has taken part in the case are present. Sometimes notes will be taken of the interrogation as it takes place, and the citizen may or may not be asked to sign them. In other cases the notes will be written up afterwards, often a matter of hours after the interrogation has taken place. In nearly every situation the notes, whether written at the time of the interview or afterwards, will be written by the officers in charge of the case and present at the interview. Rarely will the notes be made by an independent person, for rarely is such a person given the opportunity of being present at the interrogation. On some occasions the suspect will make a full confession of guilt, usually written by the police officer at the suspect's dictation, which he will then be asked to sign. Occasionally he may make a statement of his innocence.

However, whichever form is adopted (with the exception of a confession of guilt written by the suspect in his own hand) all the various forms of the interview process have one thing in common, namely to record words which at a forthcoming trial the police officer will say the citizen said. Often, if the accused pleads not guilty, he will at his trial deny saying the alleged words, or deny the alleged context in which they were said. If he has signed the notes or signed what in effect amounts to a full confession, he will often say when asked why he signed them that it was simply because he couldn't take any more of the interrogation or because the police officer told him if he didn't sign he wouldn't get bail. Obviously it follows that there are many people who when they stand trial will deliberately lie about what it is alleged they said at the police interrogation. But there are many people who when they come to stand trial cannot remember what was said with any degree of accuracy and totally deny the context of the interview as presented to the court by the police officers concerned. However the accused person puts his case at his trial, he will

6

effectively be saying that the police officers have got it wrong or that they are telling lies.

Before considering examples which may help to illustrate the situation clearly, there are certain basic principles of which the reader should be aware. Firstly the police officer knows that anything he writes down which is adverse to the citizen will be given in evidence when he stands his trial. Secondly he knows the likely effect upon ordinary people on the jury of allegations or statements he will allege the accused said. Thirdly he knows that if he alleges that the accused made certain admissions of guilt at his interview, the citizen, if he is seeking acquittal, will have to give evidence. Fourthly he knows that when giving evidence the citizen will in many cases be calling the police officer a liar, even if he doesn't use that particular word. Fifthly, if he is dealing with a man with a previous conviction, and the man accuses the police officer of telling lies, then details of that man's previous conviction go before the jury. Such is the basic knowledge which the police officer has at the time of the interrogation.

If we take a full written confession of guilt as our opening example the picture may become a little clearer. A man is arrested for a criminal offence, is taken to the police station and put in a cell. After eight hours he makes a written statement which he signs and which if true amounts to a full confession of guilt. At his trial he agrees that he made it but asserts that it simply wasn't true. He states that the reason he made it was because of threats made by the police against his family; or he says he made it because one of the police officers said he wouldn't get bail unless he did; or he says that the police officer wrote it down, not at his dictation, and he signed it because he could no longer stand the pressures of interrogation.

Now it is a fundamental rule of evidence that a confession of guilt is only admissible in evidence against a man if the confession was voluntary. Part of the theory behind this rule is that a person ought never to be forced, in a civilised society, to incriminate himself out of his own mouth unless such a confession is given voluntarily. However, we shall now see how in practice the theory collapses. In order to decide whether the confession was voluntary or not there will often be a trial in the absence of the jury before a judge alone. He will hear evidence from the police officers, who may say that the suspect was co-operative and that the confession was voluntary. The accused may say entirely the opposite. Assuming the judge is faced with two police officers of, say, 14 years and 10 years experience respectively, whom is he likely to believe? In the overwhelming majority of cases the judge will rule in favour of the police. Equally, at the trial, when the same issue is tried again, whom is an ordinary member of the public likely to believe when he starts off by believing in the impeccable integrity and virtue of police officers?

Assume that the jury have also heard that the accused has previous convictions. It is very difficult for a person with an inherent belief and trust in the police force to comprehend that behaviour by the police resulting in securing an involuntary confession is possible. Further, it must be difficult to understand what it is like to be locked in a cell for hours at a time and then to be subjected to the interrogation techniques of experienced police officers.

However, if a confession of guilt is truly voluntary, why in so many cases is a man deprived of seeing his solicitor before he makes it? (The solicitor is not allowed to prevent him from making it providing he is satisfied it is a voluntary and true confession.) Why in nearly every case is there not an independent person present when he makes it? Assume the accused is telling the truth in so far as the confession was not voluntary and in any event was not true. Is a police officer who would resort to such techniques likely to go into the witness box and say anything other than that the confession was voluntary? Is the other officer who was present, and say of an inferior rank, going to say that his superior officer behaved in anything other than the most impeccable manner? And what other evidence would an accused person have to corroborate his allegation as to the circumstances surrounding the 'confession' if there was nobody else present at the time?

Everything which has been said above concerning the 'confession' applies equally to the notes of the interrogation which the police officers allege were made at the time of the interview. The final anomaly concerns notes which the police officers write up after the interview.

Whether notes are made up at the time of an interrogation or afterwards, if they have not been signed by the accused they may not be merely read out to the court. In the majority of cases a witness is not allowed to simply read out to a court that which he has written out on an earlier occasion. The reader will thus be forgiven for thinking that if the accused does not sign the notes, what took place at the interrogation cannot be given in evidence, thus preventing a police officer from alleging matters contained within the notes which are simply not true. Regrettably the practice is entirely different, for there is another rule of evidence which allows a person when giving evidence to refresh his memory from notes which he made at the time of the alleged event, the theory being that courtroom procedure ought not to be a test of memory. This at first sight might appear reasonable. If for example one sees a motor vehicle involved in a criminal offence and makes a note of the vehicle, that is to say of its make or colour, it is only right when giving evidence at a trial many months later that you should be allowed to refresh your memory from the note which you made. However, it is not the eyewitness who regularly takes advantage of this rule but, in the overwhelming majority of cases, the police. And they take advantage of it not to refresh their memory about specific facts which they have noted but about words which they allege have been said.

Thus, to take a typical everyday example, a police officer conducts an interrogation. Thirty minutes after the interrogation has finished he writes down what has been said in his note book. This alleges that the accused made various admissions of guilt, which the accused later denies having made. When the police officer comes to give evidence some nine months later he 'refreshes his memory' from his note book, and the words that the accused is alleged to have said come flooding back to him! Further, the officer states not only that the accused said the words but also that they were said in the context alleged by the officer. The reader will readily grasp the absurdity and impossibility of the situation by asking himself whether he is able to write down with word-for-word accuracy what he read or heard thirty minutes earlier. Yet such 'evidence' is enough to make a person stand trial and in the eyes of the law is evidence upon which a reasonable jury could convict. The importance of this type of evidence will also be understood by bearing in mind the theory that in our system it is always up to the prosecution to prove guilt. It follows therefore that such evidence, however impossible it may be in reality, is sufficient to 'prove' guilt. In simple terms this means that a police allegation in court as to what a defendant said to the police is in law sufficient to prove guilt, notwithstanding the fact that the defendant may deny the allegation.

There is one other matter which is relevant at this stage. Assume that you, the reader, are on a jury. The police allege that the defendant said certain things which, if he did say them, amounted to an admission of guilt. The defendant denies saying the words alleged. You also hear that the man is a man with previous convictions. At the end of the trial you hear the learned judge in his summing up use phraseology similar to the following:

> . . . Members of the jury, the issue here is quite clear, the defendant, as you have heard, is a man with previous convictions. Merely because he has previous convictions does not mean that he is guilty of the offence for which he stands charged, neither does it mean he is incapable of telling the truth. However, when deciding whom you believe it is a matter which you can take into account, for it goes to the credit of the witness. The Crown case is supported by the accused's admissions which, according to the Crown, were made in the presence of two police officers, one a man of 14 years experience in the force and the other a man of 10 years experience. Both these officers say the admissions were made voluntarily and that the accused was co-operative. The accused on the other hand denies this and alleges what you may think amounts if true to outrageous behaviour by the officers concerned. It is entirely a question for you, members of the jury, whom you believe.

Regrettably it is a facet of human nature that when the ordinary law-abiding citizen hears that a person has been in trouble before, the seeds of an adverse reaction start to be sown. Even if this is not the case it is often very difficult to reject the inference which the judge is likely to convey in his summing-up. The relevance of this is that the police officer at the time of the interrogation knows about all these factors, including the view which the judge is likely to take if the accused does suggest that he is telling lies.

I have so far dealt with the situation in which a police officer when giving evidence states that a man made various admissions of guilt when interrogated, admissions which the accused denies having made. It only remains to touch upon the situation in which an accused person, while being interrogated by the police, makes written or oral statements consistent with his innocence. The reader ought not by now to be surprised to learn that such statements are not admissible in evidence for the purposes of proving the truth of their contents. Thus an absurd anomaly exists in which the police officer can allege that an accused while being interrogated made admissions of guilt which the jury can rely upon in order to prove guilt. The accused on the other hand cannot rely upon statements of innocence in order to prove innocence.

When, as in so many cases, there is a difference between what a police officer alleges an accused person has said while being interrogated and what the accused says he said, further prejudice is caused to an accused by the attitude of the courts to the demeanour of a witness in the witness box. Demeanour in this context simply means how a person conducts himself in the witness box. Imagine the experienced police officer who has given evidence on so many occasions. To him the witness box is 'home ground' and when he gives his evidence, as has been seen, he merely 'refreshes his memory' by reading out what he has written down on an earlier occasion, which in practice is likely to be about nine months earlier. If he is cross examined by defence counsel he merely keeps looking at his note book. Accordingly, when the question concerns the words which the officer has written down in his book, it is most unlikely that he will ever say two different things in answer to the same question.

The officer also knows from his experience the correct tone of voice to adopt when giving his evidence and the possible effects upon a jury of certain types of behaviour from the witness box.

The accused on the other hand falls into a totally different category. To him, whether or not he has been in trouble before, the witness box will be the loneliest place in the world. He does not have any notes to refer to and is often faced with having to try and remember words which he said many months earlier. Therefore the same question, if asked more than once, may produce different answers, not because he is telling lies but simply because of the context of the cross examination. He, unlike the police officer, does not have a wealth of experience behind him in giving evidence and often, though he may be totally innocent of the charge, he will adopt an attitude consistent with outraged indignation, being totally unaware that such an attitude may be giving the jury, in the cold light of a court room, the impression of arrogance. Such a person is often putty in the hands of experienced prosecuting counsel.

Although not strictly relevant to the contribution made by the police to the imprisonment of people who are or may be innocent, it is nonetheless necessary to mention the issue of complaints against the police. At the time of writing, if a person wishes to make a complaint about a policeman's behaviour it is open to him to do so. The complaint will usually be investigated by a senior officer of another branch of the force. In essence, therefore, the police investigate their own. The practice whereby one police officer investigates complaints made against another is one which has been regularly criticised on the grounds that, if such a system is to be effective, complaints against police officers should be investigated by some form of independent tribunal. While common sense and reason must dictate that it cannot be in the interests of the ordinary citizen for a police officer to investigate complaints made against one of his colleagues, I doubt whether the answer lies in the independent tribunal, for who will decide who sits upon such a tribunal? Whoever it is, what types of people will be chosen? It surely is of little use to appoint people to such a tribunal who start off with the belief that the police officer can do nothing wrong. Neither is it of any use to appoint a person who starts off antagonistic to the police. Equally the people appointed must have knowledge of the law and police procedure. I am firmly of the view that the only people who could fairly and reasonably safely be trusted to deal with complaints against the police are the same people as deal with complaints made by the police against the individual. Thus there ought to be certain kinds of conduct deemed to be unlawful for which the citizen has a remedy in damages. If a citizen alleges that he has been the victim of such conduct, then providing he can make out a prima facie case, he should be entitled to proceed against the police officer irrespective of his means. A jury would decide the merits of the case.

Observations and Remedies

It will now be evident to the reader that the number of days spent in prison by people innocent of the crime for which they have been charged, or merely arrested, must be enormous. Whether such imprisonment is the result of being arrested and released without being charged, or being charged and refused bail before subsequently being acquitted, is not relevant. The principle is that in a perfect system no innocent man should spend one day in prison before trial.

The contribution made by the police to the prevailing situation ought now to be obvious to the reader, but to point the finger of blame at the police force or at individual officers is a futile and unfair exercise, for they are human beings doing their jobs in the ways they themselves feel are best. There are policeman who are honest, virtuous men of impeccable character. There are also police officers who fall well short of such a high standard. Similarly, there are police officers who treat the whole situation as some sort of a game between them and 'the defence' with a conviction being the prize at the end of the day.

The real fault lies where it always has been: with those who are in positions of power, whether they be judges or politicians or other people holding high public office. These are people who, whatever their personal political beliefs, know from their education and experience about what goes on in practice, and have refused for one reason or another to take positive steps to rectify the situation. They have allowed a false image of the investigating police officer and the manner of police inves-

13

tigation to be presented to the unsuspecting public for fear of the consequences of the public knowing and understanding the reality of the practice. Yet it would be relatively easy to bring the practice closer to the theory.

The dangers which have been highlighted within this chapter can be avoided in the following manner: firstly, by the implementation of a rule which would make certain that a man could only be arrested for a criminal offence if at the time of his arrest there was some admissible evidence in existence of the man's guilt. If it transpired at the man's trial that in fact the police officer did not have such evidence or that there was not such evidence in existence at the time of arrest, then the accused would be entitled to have the evidence which was not in existence ruled inadmissible. This does not mean to say that merely because evidence is discovered subsequent to a man's arrest it should not be admissible against him. It only means that you ought not to be able to arrest someone and lock him up unless you have some evidence at that time of his guilt. Further, if a man is arrested without any evidence, is imprisoned and is subsequently acquitted, he should be entitled as of right to compensation. The amount should be decided by a jury. In claiming his compensation he ought to be entitled as of right to legal representation not dependent upon his income or capital. One of the consequences of adopting such a rule and giving it teeth would be that the police officer would rarely arrest a man unless he had reasonable cause – and reasonable cause would mean some evidence to place before a jury.

Secondly, a man who has been wrongfully arrested ought to be entitled as of right to demand a full public apology printed in a national newspaper by the authority which caused the prosecution to be brought or which was instrumental in collecting the evidence which resulted in such a prosecution being brought. This would go some way towards removing the cloud of suspicion which may hang over the head of the innocent man and his family after he has been acquitted and go some way towards putting him in the same position as he was in prior to being arrested.

Thirdly, there must be a recognition by those in authority that when a man is arrested and in police custody this in many ways is analogous to imprisonment without trial, that all interviews must be conducted with a solicitor present, and that the result of such interviews can only subsequently be offered in evidence if they have been tape-recorded there and then by an independent person, a copy of the tape recording being given to the accused's solicitor. This will prevent what can only be described as the farce which is regularly played out in our courts, with the police officer saying that the accused said things which the accused denies.

Fourthly, a man's previous convictions ought never to be admissible in evidence against him merely because he accuses a police officer of telling lies from the witness box or making up part of his story. This will remove the prejudicial effect of a jury having to decide who is telling the truth between a police officer and a man who has been in trouble in the past.

As with most rules, exceptions will often have to be made in order to accommodate unusual situations, for example cases which involve national security. However, enforcement of the principles behind such rules would undoubtedly go a long way towards bringing the practice of the investigating police officer into line with the ordinary law-abiding citizen's understanding of liberty and freedom. There would be far less room for manoeuvre for the unscrupulous police officer or the one who treats the whole situation as some sort of a game. The honest and fair minded police officer would be less likely to suffer because of those who do not possess such ideals or who are unscrupulous. The credibility of the police force as a whole, instead of slowly withering away, would be slowly restored, for although every democratic society requires an efficient police force to protect its law-abiding citizens, the one thing that such a society ought not to tolerate is a police force which obtains its evidence of 'guilt' against a citizen by unfair, unnecessary and underhand methods, and it can be no defence of the use of such methods that the rules of the system within which the police operate allow such methods to be used.

It is doubtful whether the reader will see any of the above remedial suggestions ever put into practice. A variety of reasons can easily be given as to why that should be so, but at the end of the day there will probably be one underlying reason more potent than any other, namely the fear of a guilty man being acquitted.

The consequences of the police force being allowed to carry on the investigative process and present their evidence against the citizen in the present manner, coupled with the contribution this makes towards innocent people being imprisoned, can be far-reaching. Any trust which such a man may have in the police force and the system as a whole is immediately replaced by mistrust and anger, a state of mind which he passes on to his children and his family, leaving him with a real sense of grievance, and without any practical right to compensation.

BAIL

The innocent man who, having been arrested and imprisoned at the police station and who has not been granted bail by the police, is then, usually within a very short period after being charged with an offence, brought before the Magistrates Court when he can apply to be released upon bail pending his trial. It is at this stage that an accused person is taken from police custody initially into the custody of the court, and whatever happens to him from now onwards he will rarely be returned to police custody. Regrettably it has been a feature of our legal system that a considerable time has often elapsed between when a person is first brought before a Magistrates Court and when he eventually stands his trial before a judge and jury at the Crown Court. Periods of eighteen months have not been uncommon in the past.

Fortunately, at the time of writing, the waiting time has been dramatically improved, but periods of up to nine months are still the rule rather than the exception. Accordingly, as in our system all people are presumed to be innocent until proven guilty and as this includes those who are in fact innocent, it would probably appear to the ordinary citizen that by granting bail the period of the innocent man's confinement in prison would be kept to a minimum. Regrettably in many cases this is not so, and often it is at this stage that the injustice already caused while the accused was in police custody is further aggravated.

A person charged with a criminal offence has basically two avenues by which he may obtain bail. Firstly he may apply to a Magistrates Court to be released on bail. Secondly if refused by the Magistrates Court he may apply to a High Court Judge in chambers. Application to the High Court Judge in chambers

17

merely means an application to a High Court Judge sitting in a private room, during which the accused has no right to be present and hear what is going on. There is also a general rule laid down by the Divisional Court of the Queens Bench Division of the High Court that in the absence of a change in circumstances a person has the right to one application and one only before the Magistrates Court, although in practice the magistrates may allow more than one application for bail if they are satisfied there is good reason for making the further application or applications. However, assuming the accused is to be eventually tried at the Crown Court before judge and jury, in the normal course of events it could be many months before he has been formally transferred from the jurisdiction of the Magistrates Court into the jurisdiction of the Crown Court. To the innocent man the application for bail is one of the most important applications he can make when he is brought before the court, further the importance of the application from a human rights angle can never be underestimated for if the application is refused it automatically leads to a substantial period of imprisonment without trial. The grant of bail is considered to be of such importance that Parliament through legislation has sought fit to enact a statute which regulates the position.

This statute clearly states that every citizen has a right to bail which can only be removed in certain specified situations, for instance when it is believed that an accused person if granted bail would fail to surrender to custody, or if granted bail would commit further offences, or if granted bail would interfere with witnesses. Further, for the Court to believe that any of these possibilities exist there must be substantial grounds placed before it. The reader could readily be forgiven for assuming that with the backing of the principles of basic human rights and the force of an Act of Parliament the period which an innocent man spends in prison awaiting his trial would be kept to the barest minimum, namely while he has been in police custody. In practice, however, because of the method by which the court applies the statute, it often becomes as impotent as a newborn baby and the reality is that in many cases a person with little money and few reputable social connections will not be granted bail if the police object.

The fact that such a practice exists can be easier understood by taking stock, at this stage, of the essential ingredients of the proceedings. The people who will decide whether or not to grant a citizen bail will either be a bench consisting of two or more magistrates, without necessarily any legal qualifications whatsoever, and who perform the work without remuneration, or a single magistrate known as a Stipendiary who will have been qualified as either a solicitor or a barrister. In both situations the magistrates will have the assistance of a clerk who is there to advise on the law if required. In neither situation does it follow that the people who will decide the issue have any experience of life in general as the ordinary man in the street understands it. The irony here is apparent when considering that following trial at the Crown Court a necessary pre-requisite of being denied one's liberty is to be found guilty by people who represent a cross section of the community and yet here, before trial, before being found guilty of any offence, and when a citizen is presumed to be innocent, his liberty can easily be taken from him by people who may not represent a cross section of the community. The police, who will usually be represented by the officer in charge of the man's case, also play a very important part in the proceedings. The state of mind of the police officer could be crucial, for he may have taken an instant dislike to the accused for any one of a variety of reasons, justified or not. The third important ingredient is the nature of the accused's representation. Often a determining factor can be the quality of the bail application itself. The individual who has little or no funds of his own will usually be granted legal aid. This, however, throughout his appearances at the Magistrates Court, will be restricted, as a general rule, to representation by a solicitor only. The solicitor is unlikely to be an experienced advocate in the same sense as a very experienced barrister, and he may have many other matters to attend to in the same court. In the alternative the solicitor may, for one reason or another, instruct a barrister to make the bail application though in such cases the barrister is likely to be very inexperienced and may at that stage be less efficient than the solicitor. It is the height of irony that when an accused person eventually stands his trial at the Crown Court he is likely to have a reasonably competent and experienced barrister to represent him, and yet at this stage of the proceedings, when his liberty is at stake without trial, rarely will he have the benefit of such representation. Those who have substantial funds of their own and who are prepared to pay can of course usually obtain the services of an experienced and competent barrister.

Having considered some of the essential ingredients present at the time when the issue of bail arises, two typical situations which occur in every day life will serve to show how the citizen can easily be denied bail. A man is involved in a fight for which, in fact, he was in no way to blame. His victim receives injuries which include cuts to his face. The police officer in charge of the case and who interviewed the suspect takes an instant dislike to him perhaps because the accused fails, in the policeman's eyes, to be as co-operative as he could be, or because of facts which have been alleged by the victim, although later it emerges that such allegations are unfounded, or for any one of a number of reasons. The accused is charged with one of the more serious of the 'assault' offences, for example wounding with intent to cause grievous bodily harm, an offence which on conviction carries with it a maximum sentence of life imprisonment. At the man's trial it is most unlikely that the indictment will contain such a serious charge, and in practice it will probably contain one of the far less serious 'assault' charges with a far less severe maximum sentence. However, this is not the trial. The police officer objects to bail, and gives as his reasons that because of the serious nature of the offence the accused would fail to surrender to custody. He goes on to say that the accused during his 'interrogation' admitted the facts which support the charge. It is most unlikely that corrobation would be required by the magistrates and bail is refused.

The reader will thus readily be able to see how easy it is to deny a person's 'right' to bail, and will understand that although the statute specifically states that the magistrates must have 'substantial grounds' for believing that the accused would fail to surrender to custody, the way in which the court interprets the statute often in reality means that 'substantial grounds' can be purely based on the police officer's opinion of the situation.

By the time the accused is committed to stand his trial, that is to say when he is transferred from the Magistrates Court to the Crown Court, which may be many months later, it becomes apparent that the initial charge is totally inappropriate, the alleged admissions consistent with guilt are totally denied, or are consistent with self defence, and the accused is granted bail.

The second typical situation involves an accused who has been in trouble in the past and who can only be described as having been a real 'villain'. However, having served his various periods of imprisonment he has at long last made a conscious effort to settle down and lead an honest life. He of course is a prime target for the police. He objects to being continually interviewed in relation to crimes in which he was not involved, and will often verbally give back to the police as good as he gets. In such a situation it only requires one unscrupulous police officer or one police officer who feels that it is part of his public duty to keep such a person off the streets, and the objections to bail become not only the possibility of failure to surrender to custody but also the possibility of the commission of further offences while on bail, the man's previous convictions being cited in support, notwithstanding the fact that he may never have failed to surrender to custody in the past or have previously committed offences while on bail.

The reader ought not to get the mistaken impression that the police always object to bail, for in a very high proportion of cases they do not. The above illustrations are typical of the many occasions on which the police do object to bail, and of the ease with which bail is often denied. Whenever bail is denied, considerable damage is being done. For a man is being kept in prison, often for substantial periods of time, without trial, on the word of a police officer and its acceptance by, in more cases than not, unqualified members of a particular sector of society. When as in many cases the accused is eventually acquitted this merely aggravates the injustice already caused. The fact that such injustice occurs is sad; the ease with which it can and undoubtedly does occur offends the inherent decency and sense of justice which the majority of people share.

I have earlier mentioned the right of a person who has been refused bail by a Magistrates Court to make an application for bail to a High Court Judge sitting in Chambers. In the opinion of the writer, such an application to a judge who may have little comparative experience in the criminal law, in secret, without an accused person having any right to attend, is a remedy against injustice unworthy of any detailed mention and affords only minimal additional protection to the innocent man imprisoned without trial.

The discussion so far has proceeded on the basis that the magistrates at least appear to comply with the recognised legal principles, but what happens if they do not? What happens if the court denies to the accused a fair and proper hearing or any hearing at all and imprisons the accused for a further period of time? Common sense may suggest to the ordinary citizen that in many cases such imprisonment would be unlawful, and that an accused would be entitled to be released by applying for the issue of one of the oldest and most famous remedies designed to protect the liberty of the subject, namely the writ of Habeas Corpus. However, this appears not to be the case, and because of a series of decisions of the Divisional Court of the Queens Bench Division, however much the Magistrates may have erred, the accused's only remedy is to apply to a High Court Judge in Chambers, whose concern will not be so much whether the magistrates acted 'lawfully' but whether in his view the accused should be granted bail. If he therefore comes to the conclusion that the accused should not be granted bail, he is in effect saying that however wrong the magistrates were in reaching their decision to refuse bail, the actual decision was right.

The absurdity of the present situation can be easily understood by considering that an accused person has the right to have his bail application decided by a Magistrates Court, and that it must follow that he has the right to have such application decided fairly and properly in accordance with the law. It is no remedy to be told by a judge that although you have been denied bail by a Magistrates Court unfairly and wrongly I, the judge wouldn't grant you bail, therefore that must be the end of the matter, for the accused didn't want the judge to consider his application in the first place. He wanted the magistrates to consider it, on the assumption that such people would be fairly representative of society at large and that such a hearing would have been fair.

Further, if at a man's trial on indictment a judge errs in law, resulting in the jury convicting, he would be entitled to appeal to the Court of Appeal for the purpose of having his conviction quashed. Rarely will a re-trial be ordered. Yet here before trial, when everybody is presumed to be innocent until a jury say otherwise, the accused can be imprisoned as a result of the magistrates acting upon a wrong principle of law, and his only remedy is to have the matter re-heard before somebody whom he didn't want to hear the application in the first place. It follows therefore that in this situation an accused person has fewer rights insofar as retaining his liberty is concerned before trial than he does when actually being tried.

An innocent person who has been denied bail and imprisoned for periods of time before trial has no right to compensation in our legal system.

Observations and Remedies

The denial of bail means imprisonment. Imprisonment before trial and imprisonment without trial are in many ways synonymous. There are those who criticise (and in the view of the writer rightly so) other legal systems in which a man may be imprisoned without being charged, or although charged, may be imprisoned without trial. Let these people demonstrate the difference between being imprisoned without being charged with an offence, and the situation which occurs in our country, where a man may be imprisoned after having been charged though the charge had little or no proper foundation in the first place. Or between the situation when a person is imprisoned for, say, six months, and then is released without a trial, and, again a situation which so often occurs in our country, when a person has been denied bail, is imprisoned for six months before being released on bail, or is never released on bail, but is tried and acquitted.

The United States of America has long recognised the importance of bail in any system which is genuinely concerned about human rights and the liberty of the individual, and only in the rarest of cases, however serious the alleged offence, will bail be denied in that jurisdiction. Also if money is to be put up to secure bail it does not necessarily have to be put up by other people in the form of 'sureties' in the way it has to in our system, for it may be that a person though innocent of any alleged offence has few friends with substantial funds who would be able, even if they were prepared, to put up the money themselves.

The fact that within our system many people having been denied bail are imprisoned and then subsequently acquitted is in the twentieth century little less than deplorable. A system which regularly allows such a situation to occur, whereby innocent people are imprisoned, and imprisoned by people without necessarily any legal qualification or without experience of life as known to ordinary people, is not a system which can be admired. The consequences to the innocent victims and their families are often enormous and are paid for in human suffering.

The remedies here are not easy, but they certainly exist. The adoption of the American system is one remedy. A Magistrates Court which may have to deal with so many other matters during the course of a day should not have important and time consuming bail applications thrust upon them at the same time. Special 'bail courts' dealing only with bail applications could easily be set up. Such courts could be manned with a mixture of people both qualified in law and unqualified, but reasonably representative of the ordinary public. All such people could be paid, thus preventing the situation where only those who could afford to take time off from work would sit. The words of the statute, whereby they must be satisfied that 'substantial grounds' exist before denying bail, ought to be given their ordinary and natural meaning, and the opinion of the police would be totally insufficient to satisfy this meaning, unless backed up by credible evidence, with the same rules of evidence applying at this stage as at a trial. For it is ridiculous that a court can deprive a man of his liberty before trial without complying with the rules of evidence, and yet be bound to comply with such rules at his trial.

The failure to rectify the situation is filling our prisons with many innocent men and propagates injustice to such an extent that the phrase human rights becomes something one merely pays lip service to.

THE PROFESSIONS

We have already seen the ease with which an innocent man may be arrested and kept in prison prior to and without trial. One of the most important factors bearing on the length of time such a person spends in prison and on the eventual outcome of his trial will be his choice of legal representation.

In the opening stages of the proceedings, which take place before the Magistrates Court prior to the accused's transfer to the Crown Court where he will stand his trial, he will in the overwhelming majority of cases be legally aided and entitled to be represented only by a solicitor, although for certain specific applications he may, though very rarely, have the right to be represented by a barrister.

Very rarely indeed will the legally-aided accused have the benefit of both a solicitor and a barrister to represent him at the Magistrates Court.

On, for example, a bail application, the likelihood of the application being successful is increased by the solicitor's advocacy; equally at the trial before a judge and jury at the Crown Court, although an accused's case will be put by a barrister, the barrister is dependent on the accused's case being properly set out in his instructions, which are drafted by the solicitor. It is therefore of the highest importance that the accused's case is fully and properly set out within the barrister's instructions and that a highly competent solicitor is chosen. It follows, therefore, that the solicitor must not only be competent and efficient but must also be the right solicitor for the particular accused, for while all solicitors have had the ability to pass the relevant examinations, complete their articles (which is another word for apprenticeship) and qualify as a solicitor, not all of them necessarily have the same experience of life, nor will they all be equally experienced in criminal matters or in advocacy. When interviewing the client one solicitor may consider that certain information given to him by the client may be totally irrelevant and needless to mention in barrister's instructions, whereas another solicitor may immediately see the significance of such information. Further, one solicitor may only be prepared to comply with the barest but essential requirements during his representation of a client whereas another may be prepared to go beyond that and often perform unpaid work and research in order to make sure that his client's case is as fully prepared as is humanly possible.

The question then arises how the innocent victim of our legal system can know who is the 'best' solicitor for his particular case? The answer is that he probably doesn't unless he has connections within the profession or has previously been in trouble so many times that he has been able to try a number of different firms of solicitors. As a general rule his choice of solicitor will often be a question of pot luck. Alternatively he will have a solicitor whom he has met in court, or if on legal aid, a solicitor who has been assigned to him by the court, or a firm of solicitors with offices near his home which he or his family have previously noticed, or the firm which previously acted for him in connection with the purchase or sale of his home. Whatever the reason for choosing any particular solicitor, in the overwhelming majority of cases it will not be because he knows that the solicitor which he has chosen is the one most able to deal properly with all the various aspects of his case.

The less able the solicitor the more likely that an innocent person will spend unnecessary time in prison. This in itself must be a sad reflection upon the difficulty of choosing the right solicitor, particularly when the stakes are so high.

For those cases, however, where trial is by judge and jury there is, in theory anyway, a type of safety valve, which while not necessarily protecting an accused person from any inadequacy of his solicitor, ought to protect him against incompetent representation on his behalf at his trial. For the representation which an accused person has at his trial will be representation by solicitor and counsel.

The counsel who represents an accused person at his trial

27

and who puts forward his case to the jury will be a person who
is qualified as a barrister-at-law. In order to become a barrister, an individual will usually have to have passed the examinations leading to a recognised law degree, and will have had
to obtain that degree to a certain minimum standard. He will
also have to have passed a number of written and practical
examinations known as the 'Bar examinations'. He is also
required to be a member of one of the four Inns of Court. These
are known respectively as Lincoln's Inn, Gray's Inn, Middle
Temple and Inner Temple. All of these Inns are situated in
the City of London and are superb buildings, steeped in tradi-
tion and history. The application form to join one of the Inns
includes a requirement for details of an individual's father and
whether he has any previous criminal convictions. A further
requirement for an individual to become a barrister is that he
dines at his Inn a certain minimum number of times. As the
reader may well imagine this requirement is often criticised
but in the view of the writer it does no harm. A person without
criminal convictions, who has passed all the relevant examinations (and of course eaten his meals!) will never be prevented
from becoming a barrister on the grounds of such matters as
religion or colour. As we shall see there is a far more subtle
method of restricting practising barristers to a certain 'type'
of person.

Having been called to the Bar, the barrister must serve a
minimum period of twelve months pupillage under a pupil
master who will be a barrister of at least five years call,
meaning that it will have been at least five years since he was
called to the bar. It doesn't follow that the pupil master will
have had at least five years practising experience although as
a general rule this will be the case. For the first six months
of the pupillage the newly qualified barrister will often follow
his master around the courts, sitting behind him during his
cases and seeing what goes on. During this period he is not
allowed to represent people on his own but during his second
six months he can. During the second six months of his pupillage he will often have the opportunity of appearing for clients
at the Magistrates Court, still in theory under the supervision
of his pupil master although in practice rarely will the pupil
master be with him. Thus although he can often seek advice

and guidance from his pupil master after he has appeared for a client he is rarely if ever given this guidance while he is actually 'on his feet' before the court in the opening stages of his career, and for all intents and purposes he is forced into having to learn many of the arts and skills of advocacy from his own mistakes.

Without having completed his pupillage a barrister, although qualified, can never practice. A barrister does not have any right to pupillage. Whether he is given it depends entirely upon the discretion of the particular barrister to whom he applies. There are some barristers who for various reasons have never taken a pupil. The newly qualified barrister with strong family or personal connections within the legal profession generally will not have much difficulty in obtaining pupillage; at the other end of the scale the newly qualified barrister without any connections, who comes from an ordinary working class background, may have great difficulty. The reader drawing on his experience of life will form his own conclusions when the situation arises that the newly qualified barrister from a working class background also happens to be a coloured boy applying to a predominantly white Bar.

Having completed his pupillage the next hurdle a barrister has to face is to find somewhere from which he can practice. Barristers practice from a set of chambers. Chambers is another word for offices. The majority of barristers who regularly appear in the courts within the London area and its surrounding borders have 'offices' within the grounds of one of the four Inns of Court. They will usually share their own room with one or more other barristers. A number of these rooms will make up what can loosely be called a suite of offices which together is referred to as a set of chambers. Many sets of chambers will have as their head a barrister who will also be a Queens Counsel, and all sets of chambers must have at least one clerk, for a barrister is not allowed to practice unless he has a clerk. The barrister therefore has to apply successfully to join one of these sets of chambers. There are sets of chambers which are very busy ones with a lot of work, and at the other end of the scale there are sets which are very quiet and which are struggling to survive. As the reader will soon become aware it does not follow that the very busy sets necessarily have a better or more able compliment of barristers. The barrister with strong connections in the legal profession will often have little difficulty in joining a 'good' set of chambers. Thus for example the barrister whose father happens to be a solicitor who regularly sends work to a particular set of chambers, or the barrister who is related to a judge, or the barrister with strong political connections or social connections within the aristocracy is likely to encounter very few problems. Often, after completing his pupillage, he will be offered a permanent position within that particular set of chambers. The barrister without any of the above or similar connections is in a totally different position and his chances of practising at any 'good' set of chambers are often minimal; further his chances of joining a comparatively quiet set are not much better, and even if he does manage to get into such a set his chances of developing a successful practice are remote. However, it is worth mentioning at this stage that many of the recognised 'good' sets of chambers will often have one female member, one coloured member and one person who is of a religion other than Roman Catholic or Church of England, out of a complement often greater than fifteen barristers.

It is at this stage that people whom the established members of the Bar consider as being undesirable in some way or another are weeded out. The fact that the individual concerned may have studied long and hard, passing all the numerous examinations required of him, or that his family may have worked for many years, doing without many of the luxuries of life in order that their child may have the benefit of a sound education, are matters which now fade into comparative insignificance. The few who do manage to 'slip through the net' then usually meet the next hurdle, one which to many proves insurmountable, namely money.

A barrister will undertake work which will be paid for either privately by the lay client or by the Government under the legal aid scheme. If the barrister is to be paid privately then his fee is negotiated between his clerk and his instructing solicitors. The barrister, unlike the solicitor, has no legal right to sue for his fees. As the reader will recall, from the time a person is arrested until his eventual trial before judge and jury there is an intermediate stage which takes place at the

The Professions

Magistrates Court, called the committal for trial, whereby the accused is transferred from the jurisdiction of that court to the jurisdiction of the Crown Court. The barrister receives his fees firstly following the committal and secondly following the trial. There will often be a number of barristers representing an accused person at the various stages of the proceedings, but as a general rule there will only be one cheque made payable to one barrister after the committal proceedings and similarly after the trial. That barrister is then expected to pay out of the cheque which he receives the money due to other barristers for the work which they performed. If the work is privately paid and the solicitor is dilatory in paying the barrister, notwithstanding the fact that as a general rule he himself would have been paid, the duty of the barrister's clerk is to chase the solicitors for the fees outstanding. However the fees outstanding may be fees due to a comparatively new member of chambers by a solicitor who sends a lot of work to that set of chambers. Often the clerk will be reluctant to chase the new member's fees with any real vigour for fear of upsetting the solicitor and prejudicing the amount of work the chambers as a whole will receive. Even when the barrister's fees are paid directly by the Government there is often a delay while the legal aid fund awaits the bill from the solicitors for their fees. It follows therefore that there is often a substantial period of time between a barrister performing a piece of work and getting paid for it, if he gets paid at all. For there are members of the bar who, having been paid for a piece of work (which included work which another barrister performed) do not voluntarily pay that other barrister, and would consider it 'ungentlemanly' conduct if asked for payment. Thus there are many barristers who have received money due to other barristers and who simply do not pay them. Further, there are firms of solicitors who, having received money due to a barrister for his fees, will keep such money on deposit as long as they possibly can, keeping the interest for themselves. On average a barrister can expect to wait between six and twelve months for his fees, if he gets them at all, and to wait up to four years is not uncommon.

The individual from an ordinary background who has managed to surmount all the various obstacles thus finds that

31

in order to survive he must have a substantial amount of capital or be able to borrow in order to survive, not because he may not be working or may be learning his trade but simply because he is not being paid with reasonable speed or is not being paid at all for work which he has performed.

This does not mean to say that there are no members of the Bar who earn substantial amounts of money. On the contrary there are many barristers who do earn what the average member of the public would consider to be a substantial annual income from their respective practices. However, the overwhelming majority of those who do earn such sums do so as a result of some form of specialised civil practice. The important point here is that no barrister, other than one appointed to the ranks of Queen's Counsel, whose practice is exclusively devoted to representing people who are accused of committing criminal offences and who is dependent on 'legal aid' for payment ever has the opportunity of earning such substantial sums however good a lawyer he may be.

I have mentioned earlier that an accused person may at the various stages of the proceedings which lead up to his trial be represented by a number of different barristers. However, in theory, for his trial he is entitled to the barrister of his choice, subject to the barrister's fee being agreed and the barrister being available. For the purposes of this book many of the clients will be legally aided and as the majority of barristers who practice in the courts of criminal law undertake legal aid work the fee is rarely a problem. When it comes to availability a different situation occurs, for in many criminal cases neither the barrister nor the solicitor nor the accused will know the exact day he is to be tried until the night before. When the trial takes place the barrister may be and often is involved in another trial somewhere else. An accused person will often have seen his counsel in conference before his trial, will have confided in him and have been given a sense of confidence by him, the barrister may have put in many hours of work preparing the case and yet on the day of the trial the accused person suddenly finds himself being represented by another barrister whom he has never met and who probably only knew about the case the night before!

It will be apparent to the reader that for an individual who wishes to become a barrister, the opportunity of establishing himself within his chosen career will often have little to do with merit. The relevance of the situation in the present context is twofold.

Firstly the overwhelming majority of judges are appointed from people who were previously barristers: and often the summing up by the judge to the jury at the end of a trial can have an important bearing upon the verdict which is eventually returned.

Secondly, in criminal cases, unlike civil cases, for a person to be found guilty he must not only have done the act in question but he must have done it in a particular state of mind. A barrister who is representing a person who denies the state of mind in question ought, if he is doing his job properly, to put his client's state of mind to the jury. In many cases, before he is able to do this, he will need to have some experience of the situations that the particular person whom he represents may have found himself involved in during his life and which may have contributed to the state of mind alleged by the accused. A barrister who comes from a comparatively ordinary working class or middle class background will often be better equipped to do this than the barrister who comes from a comparatively privileged sphere of society.

An accused who has not been able to choose the 'right' type of solicitor to prepare his case will be less likely to find the 'right' type of barrister to represent him at his trial, even if the particular barrister chosen is available on the day of the trial, for an individual apart from one exceptional situation is not allowed to instruct a barrister directly. It must always be a solicitor who instructs the barrister on his behalf. The highly competent and efficient solicitor who always uses his best endeavours for his client will if he is fortunate enough to know well in advance the date of his client's trial (this happens when the date has earlier been fixed by agreement with all parties and the trial court has agreed to have the case listed as a fixture) pick a suitable barrister. In cases where he is only likely to know the date the night before the trial takes place, he will choose a particular barrister in a set of chambers where he has confidence in a number of the members of the set, so that if the barrister chosen is not available on the particular date, hopefully one of the other members will be. At least such a solicitor is doing his best for his client. Further, this type of solicitor, when instructed privately by his client, will nearly always try to see that the barrister is paid for his work as speedily as possible. The solicitor, however, who falls short of this standard will often send his client's case to a set of chambers merely because he happens to be friendly with one of the members, or the clerk to those chambers, and will often adopt the attitude that any barrister who is sent is acceptable. Further his typed instructions will often be limited to the barest details and many relevant points will have been overlooked.

A further restriction on an accused person finding the right type of barrister for his particular case lies in the fact that there are a very large number of academically exceptional barristers who, when they become established in practice, specialise in branches of the law other than crime, thus further restricting the number of barristers available to an accused person in the first place. These barristers often tend to look down on the ones who practice exclusively in criminal law, usually on the basis that the subject is not as academically stimulating as their own. It has for a long time been an accepted fact amongst many that those whose ambitions lie in eventually becoming a Queens Counsel or a High Court Judge stand a much better chance if they excel in some subject other than criminal law. This is most regrettable for the practice of criminal law gives a much greater breadth of experience. The civil lawyer often knows the case he has to meet and the numerous issues of fact which make up that case well before he gets to court. A vast majority of civil cases never get to court at all and when they do, only in the rarest of cases is a civil lawyer faced with a jury as well as a judge. At the end of the day the issue in civil cases is usually one of money. In the majority of criminal cases prosecuting counsel does not know the case he has to meet until he gets to court and the case which defence counsel has to meet may vary depending upon the prosecuting witnesses. The advocate who appears in a criminal case is required not only to know the criminal law but also the law of evidence. He is required to master the techniques of examination and cross examination of witnesses as well as the different methods of communicating not merely with the judge but also with the jury. He has to have some understanding of human nature as well as being a reasonably efficient speechmaker. Most of all, what is at stake in a criminal trial is the liberty of the subject. The barrister who specialises in the courts of criminal law and who regularly has to think on his feet making split-second decisions connected with the conduct of his case often faces a far more demanding task than that faced by the civil lawyer.

It is not possible to finish this chapter without mentioning the issue of disciplinary proceedings against members of the professions. Complaints brought against solicitors will be investigated by a tribunal which contains qualified solicitors. Complaints brought against barristers will be investigated by a tribunal which contains a number of barristers as well as a few 'lay' members and will be presided over by a High Court Judge. Complaints brought against solicitors do not require detailed mention in a book of this nature, for, the innocent man, in cases where trial is by judge and jury, will have dual protection including representation by counsel, so complaints against barristers are more particularly relevant here. A barrister who fails properly and adequately to put forward his client's case can expect to be severely dealt with, if his lay client or solicitor have a justified complaint, the ultimate sanction being disbarment, preventing the barrister from practising.

However, the tribunal can and in a large number of cases is put to a far more subtle use, namely to deal with complaints brought against a barrister, usually defence counsel, not by his lay client or by his instructing solicitor but by a judge. The dangers in this type of situation are obvious; for often when a complaint is brought by a judge against a barrister which is to be investigated by a tribunal presided over by another judge who may be of the same standing as the judge who made the complaint there can only be one winner. If the tribunal were to hold otherwise there would be the inference that the judge was wrong and the barrister was justified in whatever conduct led to the complaint. This can be a very useful method of preventing a barrister from practising, whose only real 'crime' may be that because of his background and attitudes he believes in a different approach from that of the judge who made the complaint. When a barrister is deprived of his profession it follows so far as the criminal law is concerned that the public are also deprived of a particular type of person to represent them. It may be that the public would consider such action by the tribunal in a given situation perfectly justified, but surely it ought to be for them to decide. That a barrister can be found 'guilty' of an offence without being given the opportunity of trial by jury ought not to be tolerated, for the situation which exists will often give to a barrister less rights than we give to any other type of person accused of a criminal offence, and in many cases produces far more disastrous consequences if the allegation is found to be proved.

Observations and Remedies

An individual who passes all the required examinations and who can properly call himself a barrister should not have to depend on some other person, who may come from a totally different background, condescending to give him the opportunity to pupillage before he is allowed to practise. The giving of pupillage ought to be a duty other members of the profession are obliged to carry out, whether they want to or not, and whatever their personal views of the background of any individual pupil. Before a barrister is allowed to represent people in the courts it ought to be essential for him to have had a minimum period of practical experience under the direct supervision of his master. Thus if he is in court with his master he should be allowed, with the consent of the lay client, to develop the basic techniques of asking questions. Properly controlled, it is doubtful if this could prejudice the lay client, for the jury, who would have earlier been informed, would readily understand that this is a novice learning his trade.

It cannot possibly be right for other barristers, when deciding whether to take on a 'newcomer', to be looking, consciously or otherwise, for an individual who comes from a similar background to themselves, for this merely continues restricting the Bar to the privileged few. However, it is a natural facet of human nature that if a person has certain prejudices, whether they be against colour, race, religion or social background, you cannot force them by laws or rules to change their basic attitudes (something which Parliament has yet to learn). Only the experience of finding good things in the types of people they have previously criticised will bring about a change in attitude.

A barrister who has performed work ought never to be prevented from receiving the fees rightfully due to him and ought to be entitled to be paid directly within the shortest possible time, whether such payment is made by his instructing solicitor or by the Government. A solicitor who has been paid the barrister's fees by his client and who deliberately witholds payment of those fees to the barrister while earning interest upon it himself ought to be accountable to the barrister not only for the fees and any interest earned by the solicitor but also for any loss the barrister may have suffered while being deprived of his fees, and like every other member of the community the barrister ought to be entitled to sue for money rightfully due to him which he has not received.

For many hundreds of years the ordinary member of the public arrested and charged with any one of the majority of criminal offences has had the right to be tried by other members of the public, namely before a jury. A jury usually consists of people drawn from various walks of life who bring into a court room their own common sense, which they have acquired from their own personal experiences of life. Such people ought not to be prevented from having a substantial number of their 'own kind' available to represent them should they find themselves victims of the legal system, and they should be able to choose the person they feel most suitable to represent them, providing such a person has satisfied the minimum education requirements. Once a barrister has qualified it ought never to be possible to deprive him of his calling without him having the right to trial by jury, for it ought to be up to the people to say whether the person in question is a fit and proper person to carry on representing them.

In the view of the writer, the only way there is likely to be any significant change in the present system is by adopting a system similar to that which prevails in the United States of America. Certainly, so far as the criminal law is concerned, a merger of the professions in some form or other would be essential. There ought to be a simple category known as trial lawyer and the moment a person has qualified to this level and had sufficient experience he ought to be entitled to open an office on his own, assisted by his clerk or secretary. Members of the public ought to be entitled to seek his advice directly. For the seeds of any such system to be given the opportunity of successful growth the courts would have to start putting the interests of an accused individual, who is presumed to be innocent, first, before their own administrative problems, and should always be ready to assist in fixing specified dates for trials in advance. The trial lawyer would then be able to plan his work in advance, and the accused person would be reasonably certain of the availability of the person whom he wishes to represent him, without finding himself being represented by a totally new person, whom he has never previously met, on the morning of the trial.

THE COURTS

An individual who has been arrested and charged with a criminal offence has the option, as a general rule, of being tried in either of two courts. These two courts are the Magistrates Court and Crown Court. Trial at the Crown Court is before judge and jury, except when a person is appealing to the Crown Court from his conviction by the Magistrates Court, in which case there is no jury. There is no jury in the Magistrates Court. The general rule is subject to a number of important exceptions. Firstly very serious offences such as Murder, Rape, Robbery can only be tried at the Crown Court before judge and jury. Secondly there are a large number of less serious offences which can only be tried at the Magistrates Court, and the accused person is thus deprived of being tried by a jury. These offences include not only many of the motoring offences but also allegations of assault on police officers and many offences in connection with the receipt of social security benefits and related matters. Thirdly there is also a very large number of offences which can be tried either in the Magistrates Court or before a jury at the Crown Court. In order for the magistrates to try such a case they require the consent of the accused and they must also agree to try the case, something which unless the prosecution object is often a mere formality.

As in many cases an accused person's consent is required before he can be tried in a Magistrates Court, thus depriving him of a jury, this becomes a very important decision for an accused person to make, and often he will rely on advice from his legal advisers. In the overwhelming majority of cases in which the accused has been granted legal aid he is restricted to advice from a solicitor only. This is often regrettable because there can be a personal interest to the solicitor in seeing that his client is tried in the Magistrates Court. This interest arises because a solicitor has a right of audience in the Magistrates Court and could act as advocate for an accused person in such a court, whereas in the Crown Court he does not have such a right, that being the province of a barrister.

There are certain theoretical advantages in being tried in the Magistrates Court. For example, a person without any previous convictions could usually expect a lower sentence if he pleads guilty to or is found guilty of an offence in such a court. The person who wishes to get the whole matter disposed of as speedily as possible will often find the process much quicker (and often be more likely to be convicted), than having to await his trial at the Crown Court. In the overwhelming majority of cases, however, there are far greater disadvantages in trial by the magistrates, and the following matters should always be taken into account.

Firstly the magistrates have substantial powers of imprisonment. Thus, for example, a person who is charged with two or more offences can be given an immediate custodial sentence by the magistrates of up to twelve months imprisonment.

Secondly, if the individual who has been in trouble before and acquired a previous conviction is found guilty and they wish to give him a greater sentence than that which they have power to impose, the magistrates could commit the individual to the Crown Court for sentence. By this method a person could receive a substantially greater sentence of imprisonment without ever having his guilt determined by a jury.

Thirdly, for a person to be convicted by a jury, initially all twelve members must agree, and if they are unable to reach agreement after having deliberated for a period in excess of two hours, at least ten of them must agree before they are able to convict (providing the jury still consists of at least eleven members). In the Magistrates Court trial will either be before one single stipendiary magistrate or two or three lay magistrates. Very rarely will more than three magistrates sit in order to decide guilt.

Fourthly, the ordinary citizen when being tried in the Magistrates Court is rarely going to be tried by his 'peers', for the magistrates will often come from a different sphere of society to himself.

Fifthly, as regards future consequences to a person's character, if he is convicted, the law does not draw any distinction between a person who has been found guilty at a Magistrates Court and one who has been found guilty at the Crown Court.

Sixthly, once a person has elected for trial at the Magistrates Court, only in the rarest of circumstances is he allowed to change his mind. It follows, therefore, that once an accused person has decided to be tried by the magistrates he forfeits his right to jury trial. Even if having been convicted he appeals on the basis that he was not guilty and wrongly convicted, on his appeal, which will often involve a full re-hearing of the facts, he will still be denied a jury.

There is also a very important difference between the procedure which takes place in the Magistrates Court and the one which takes place in the Crown Court, as a result of which great prejudice can easily be caused to the innocent man. In the Crown Court the defendant and his representatives will have received well in advance copies of the statements of the prosecution witnesses (with the possible exception of the accused's counsel who as we have seen may not have received them until the night before). The accused will therefore have had the opportunity of seeing the case which is alleged against him before he stands his trial. He will have had the opportunity to discuss points contained in it with his solicitor, and to obtain any of his own witnesses who could rebut certain parts of the prosecution case. However, in the Magistrates Court, the accused and his representative, often just a solicitor, do not have any right to see in advance the statements made by the prosecution witnesses and they can easily be, and often in fact are, taken completely by surprise, by for example, a relevant accusation which though totally unfounded they were not prepared for. The accused does not have the opportunity to discuss such an allegation with his solicitor because he does not know of its existence and would find difficulty in discussing it with him at the time, when he would be in the dock and his solicitor may be 'on his feet'.

The overwhelming majority of people who sit as magistrates, with the exception of those who are known as Stipendiary Magistrates, do not possess any legal qualifications whatsoever, although they have a clerk to advise them on the law.

Further, they do not have any practical experience consistent with membership of the legal professions. They are unpaid for their work as magistrates and thus in many cases are people who can regularly afford to take time off work or who have no need to work at all.

In the Crown Court trial will be before judge and jury, apart from those cases where a person is appealing from a conviction at the Magistrates Court, in which case the whole matter will be re-heard at the Crown Court but without a jury. However long the innocent man has spent waiting for his trial, whether he has been on bail or in prison, in theory his eventual protection lies before a jury chosen at random from ordinary people taken from different walks of life and with a judge, a person of the highest integrity, totally unbiased towards the proceedings, there to direct the jury upon the law and to see that fair play takes place between the accused and the Crown. A different picture, however, emerges in practice, which the reader will observe when he considers, in the next chapter, the very important part which the judge actually plays.

Observations and Remedies

It cannot possibly be right for people without any legal qualifications or experience, and who are often unrepresentative of society, to be given the power to act as judge and jury and to have the capacity to impose immediate sentences of imprisonment for substantial periods of time. Neither can it be right for a person to be forcibly deprived of a trial by jury, as in those cases when he has no such right, and yet be liable not only to immediate imprisonment but also to the loss of his good character.

In the present system of Magistrates Court proceedings the advantages to Government and the police are numerous, whereas the advantages to the individual are few. Trial at the Magistrates Court is a very cheap method of 'justice' when compared with trial at the Crown Court. Those who in the majority of cases are responsible for the prosecutions which are brought in the Magistrates Court know well in advance that the people who will be trying the case will be representative not of society generally, but often of those in positions of power, and thus are far more likely to share a similar attitude with the prosecuting authority than with any other branch of society drawn at random, for magistrates are appointed, directly, indirectly or as a result of recommendations, by those who hold high positions of public office. Actions for offences involving allegations of an assault upon the police, which common sense ought to dictate should be tried before a jury, may never be tried before a jury, thus making it much easier for the police to obtain a conviction and much more difficult for an innocent man ever to be acquitted. It is also accepted by many lawyers that in the overwhelming majority of cases an innocent man stands a far better chance of being acquitted at the Crown Court than he ever does before a Magistrates Court.

Perhaps one of the few real advantages of the proceedings within the Magistrates Court, so far as an accused person is concerned, comes when he wishes to plead guilty to an offence of a comparatively minor nature. Even if he has previous convictions there is still only the remotest possibility that the magistrates would commit him to the Crown Court for sentence.

Some of the remedies which would help to ensure a reasonable degree of fair play at the Magistrates Court are far from difficult to invoke. Firstly, magistrates ought to be paid, and should be drawn from the various sectors of society, thus preventing the situation when only those who can afford to be magistrates will be magistrates. Secondly, there should be not less than five magistrates sitting whenever a person is to be tried for a criminal offence, and included in those five ought to be a qualified solicitor or barrister. A verdict of guilty ought only to be returned if the magistrates are unanimous. This would go part of the way towards making sure that there is a real similarity between jury trial and trial by the magistrates. Thirdly, no individual who stands in jeopardy of losing his good character should ever be deprived of jury trial. Fourthly, differentiation ought to exist between a conviction obtained at the Magistrates Court after a trial without a jury, and one obtained at the Crown Court before a jury, with far less weight being attributed to the former.

THE JUDGE

Rarely can there have been an office which commands more respect than that of the judge. To the layman his character and integrity are beyond reproach, his learning and wisdom equate with those of a Solomon, his ability to be unbiased and fair to all parties is instinctive and he can always be trusted to ensure that an accused person receives a fair trial and that an innocent man will never be wrongly convicted. Such at least is the picture which the law abiding citizen is brought up, from the earliest years, to believe in. The reality of the situation will soon become apparent, but before we take a closer look at the role which the judge actually plays it is necessary to mention that there are judges both past and present who have either reached or come fairly close to the standards expected of them by the law abiding public. The tragedy is that while all judges are people of good character, many fall far short of the picture which has been painted of them. The reasons for such a sorry state of affairs will soon become fairly obvious.

There are various different categories of judges but for the purposes of this book only two are relevant. These are the judges who are called High Court Judges but who do occasionally sit in the Crown Court, and those other judges who regularly sit in the Crown Court but who have not been elevated to the status of a High Court Judge. Rarely, other than on a charge of murder, will an accused person be tried by a High Court Judge sitting with a jury, and in the overwhelming majority of cases he will be tried by an ordinary Crown Court Judge who sits in the Crown Court week after week or moves around between different Crown Courts. As it is he who in all

45

probability will be the judge at a person's trial, it is he with whom we are most concerned.

In order to become a judge a man's willingness so to serve has to be made known to the Lord Chancellor, an office which in itself is a political appointment, but what criterion is adopted in deciding suitability is somewhat shrouded in secrecy. History shows, however, that the vast majority of judges were previously barristers. The fact that most judges were previously barristers is a factor which has often come in for considerable criticism, and yet it must surely be essential for a judge to know the skills and tricks of the advocate if he is to act as an umpire between two advocates at a trial. However, far more to the point is that before being appointed a judge and being allowed to try a criminal matter in the Crown Court, he need not necessarily have practised as a barrister at the criminal bar. His previous practice may have been mainly of a civil nature, he need never have been a successful practising barrister, and he need not necessarily have a law degree conferred from one of the major universities or even have passed any examinations upon the law of evidence. Of prime importance, his experience of life in general may be very limited.

By appointing judges primarily from the Bar, the types of people who will become judges must necessarily be restricted to those who are in that particular profession, and we have already seen that the profession is totally unrepresentative of ordinary people at large. It must follow that judges will in all probability be even more unrepresentative. Accordingly, at the very beginning of a trial the mind of a judge is likely to differ substantially from the minds of the jury on the interpretation of matters which occur in everyday life, and as at most criminal trials many of the issues involved are issues of fact or the inferences which are to be drawn from those facts, an inbuilt bias against the defendant can easily occur before the trial has even begun, for in many cases the judge will have taken the opportunity to read the papers on the trial before the trial begins.

Prior to the commencement of a trial, judges, unlike members of a jury, will often know whether or not an accused person has previous convictions. It is the height of irony that while in many cases a jury of ordinary citizens will not know of an accused's previous convictions for fear of prejudice, the legal system sees nothing wrong in the person who will eventually have to direct them on the law and sum up the evidence to them knowing about such convictions particularly when the final words from such a person could carry great weight with the jury.

Many of the judges who have previously been practising barristers at the Criminal Bar have often concentrated mainly on prosecuting, and the success of their practices has often been due to the predominance of prosecuting work; they may never have had a successful defence practice. It is difficult to understand how a person who has never possessed a successful practice defending people, which will often regularly involve putting forward the state of mind of an accused, can successfully give the same amount of weight to both sides of a story.

A person appointed to the position of a judge in many ways begins upon a new career. If he is ambitious he may well have his sights upon being appointed a High Court Judge, or on sitting in the Court of Appeal or eventually the Lords. Those who have to decide upon his suitability for promotion will obviously consider his performance up to that date. It would be the height of naivety to consider, all other factors being equal, that a person in whose court there had been an unusually high number of acquittals would be looked upon with equal favour as one in whose court there had been a reasonable number of convictions. A judge who allows a factor such as promotion to weigh upon his mind will often be looking for proof positive of innocence as the alternative to believing in the guilt of the accused.

A judge who forms the opinion that an accused person is guilty, notwithstanding the fact that he may in reality be innocent, will often bring pressure to bear upon his counsel if the accused person has a barrister who believes in his client and the principles of his own calling sufficiently to put his client's case in the strongest or most appropriate manner. There are many methods by which the judge is able to do this, for example if defence counsel wants time in which to consider a particular point the judge will suggest that he does so over the luncheon adjournment; or if counsel has had a particularly long and arduous day cross examining the prosecution witnesses and only a few minutes remain of the court day, the judge will order defence counsel to commence the defence case there and then, instead of allowing him overnight to recall his thoughts. Or the judge might call upon defence counsel to make his closing speech right at the end of a day, thus preventing him from using the evening in which to refresh his memory.

The subtle smiles to the jury at various stages throughout a man's trial, conveying to the jury the judge's opinion of the defendant's counsel or of the point which he may have been trying to make; calling defence counsel to his private room on the basis that he has observed some technical fault or defect in counsel's conduct; reminding counsel of his own personal powers and enquiring who is the head of the particular barrister's chambers: these are but a few of the more common examples. To stand up to a judge knowing full well that such conduct may seriously damage his career may require certain strengths which the barrister in question may not possess.

The defence counsel who trys to put his client's case as strongly and as forcibly as he can, assuming that the case is of a type which merits such an approach, will often find himself against not only the prosecution but the judge as well, and will often be putting his own career on the line whenever he enters a courtroom.

Right near the end of a person's trial, after counsel for the prosecution and counsel for the defence have made their closing speeches to the jury, the judge then directs them as to the law and sums up the evidence for both the prosecution and the defence. It is not for the judge to tell the jury one way or the other what their verdict should be, and he will not do so directly. In many cases, the technique which the judge adopts will, however, leave the jury in very little doubt as to what verdict the judge considers appropriate and when this occurs, rarely (never in the writer's experience) is he conveying to them that an acquittal is the appropriate verdict.

This technique is comparatively simple. The judge will always preface his summing up to the jury by informing them that, whatever he says about the facts, if the jury believe something different to him it is their decision which matters. Now, many of the members of the jury may not at that stage have formed an opinion one way or the other and are looking to the judge for assistance. It may be useful to consider a number of typical examples of this technique at work. Assume that you, the reader, are sitting upon a jury trying any one of the following cases. (All characters are fictitious.)

Case 1   A case of shoplifting

Mrs Smith, a middle aged lady of fifty-five years of age who has never been in any trouble before, is arrested and charged with theft in circumstances which amount to shoplifting.

The evidence for the prosecution at the trial is that Mrs Smith was seen walking around one of the big stores in a suspicious manner. She was then seen to pick up various items, including hair spray and toilet commodities, off the counter. The total value of the items was just under ten pounds. She was then seen to walk straight past the cash desk and through the main doors leading to the street whereupon she was arrested by the store detective.

While giving evidence the store detective states that when he arrested Mrs Smith and confronted her with the facts she failed to give any explanation for her conduct other than to say she was sorry, and was found to be in possession of over fifty pounds in cash. Two police officers, who had been called by the store manager, give evidence that Mrs Smith had said to them that she had never done anything like this before and begged them not to prosecute.

The only evidence called by the defence is Mrs Smith, who admits that she took the items in question but had done so in a moment of absent-mindedness, and, further, she could not remember, due to the lapse of time between her arrest and her trial, what she had said to the police. Mrs Smith is strongly cross examined by prosecuting counsel and, as she is not a 'professional witness' used to giving evidence, is obviously a bag of nerves. This factor alone not unnaturally can produce an adverse reaction to her evidence.

After hearing speeches from counsel for the prosecution and

counsel for the defence your mind is undecided and the issue is evenly balanced. The judge directs you upon the law, referring to genuine absent mindedness as a defence because it negates the intent which is required on a charge of theft, and reminding you that before you convict you have to be sure of a person's guilt, and then he sums up to you in the following terms:

'. . . Mr Thomas, a supervisor of the store, which is probably well known to you, has given evidence that he first saw Mrs Smith walking in a suspicious manner near the stand which sells ladies' hairspray and related commodities, whereupon he saw Mrs Smith take the items, which form the subject matter of this charge, and put them in her white plastic carrier bag. She then walked straight past the cash desk without, so it would appear, pausing for a second, and by the defendant's own admission did not pay for any of the goods. Mrs Brown, who, as you have heard, is a very experienced store detective, having been employed by the store for a period in excess of ten years, challenged Mrs Smith outside the store, on the pavement, where she said that Mrs Smith immediately admitted that she had taken the goods and had done so without paying. You then heard the evidence of two police officers who had been called to the store, both of whom have a wealth of experience in the police force. According to both these officers – and it has not been challenged by the defence – Mrs Smith repeated the admissions she had made to the store detective, namely that she had taken the goods and had not paid for them and begged them not to prosecute her. At that stage, members of the jury, there had been no mention whatsoever of what she now tells you in court. There is one other matter, members of the jury, which you may think to be of importance, namely that shoplifting is a serious offence, for its consequences are that most of us have to pay increased prices for those goods which we lawfully wish to purchase, and although you must only convict the defendant if you are satisfied so that you are sure of her guilt, in reaching your verdict you must put aside sentimental or emotional considerations and reach it according to the evidence. A person charged with a criminal offence is not in our system obliged to give evidence. That person can sit back and do nothing at all, making the prosecution prove their case, but if he does give evidence then such evidence forms part of the evidence in the case as a whole. Mrs Smith gave evidence. It is for you to decide what weight you attach to it. You are entitled to take into account a person's demeanour when they give evidence, that is to say how they conduct themselves in the witness box. You saw Mrs Smith in the witness box, you heard her give her evidence. The question you have to ask youself is whether you feel that she is being totally frank and honest about the situation; and you will recall that while she said she never intended not to pay for the goods she has not given any explanation as to why she did not say anything about absent mindedness to anybody at the time of her arrest. But of course it is entirely a question for you, members of the jury, what weight you attach to her evidence. . . .'

Assuming that your state of mind was perfectly evenly balanced before listening to the judge's summing up, would it still be as evenly balanced now?
Now compare the above 'not untypical' summing up with the following summing up which is far from the norm.

'. . . Now bearing in mind what I have said to you about the law in this case it is necessary to examine the evidence. None of the evidence which the prosecution have led in this case has been challenged by the defence and it is common ground that there is no dispute that Mrs Smith did take the goods in question and did not in fact pay for them, but that is not the issue. The real issue is the state of mind that Mrs Smith had when she passed through the gangway leading to the cash desk and passed by the cash desk. In order for you to convict Mrs Smith of this offence you must be satisfied that she was acting dishonestly with the intention to permanently deprive the store of their goods. If for some reason, because of other matters which might have been weighing upon her mind, she was merely forgetful or absent minded and had not formed the required dishonest intent then she is not guilty of the offence. Similarly, if you are not sure, it would be your duty to acquit. Mrs Smith gave evidence in the case, when she totally denied that she had ever formed the dishonest intention of depriving the store of their goods without paying for them. You have heard that she is a woman of previous good character, which is something you can take into account when considering her evidence. You may have observed that Mrs Smith appeared frightened when giving her evidence. You may think that it would be wrong to attach too much weight to that fact, for a person can appear to be frightened because they have a nervous disposition which can easily be brought about by giving evidence. It is a well accepted fact that the witness box can often seem the loneliest place in the world. . . .'

Case 2   A case of armed robbery

Roger Thomas, a person with previous convictions for offences of burglary and one previous conviction for an offence of armed robbery some seven years ago, is arrested and charged with an offence of armed robbery upon a security van, when a shotgun was discharged seriously wounding a security guard in the leg. The Crown's case against Mr Thomas is based upon three eye witnesses to the robbery, who give evidence to the effect that all the robbers wore stocking masks and gloves and two of them were of a similar height to Mr Thomas, and three detectives, who give evidence to the effect that when Mr Thomas was shown a statement made by a Mr Johnson, a person who had pleaded guilty to the robbery, which incriminated Mr Thomas, and was asked whether the facts within that statement were true, he answered yes. Mr Johnson does not give evidence.

Mr Thomas totally denies the charge and denies making admissions of guilt as alleged by the police. He does not, however, give evidence from the witness box because he knows that if he does he will effectively have to call the police liars or to inform the jury that the reason why Mr Johnson may have alleged those matters in his statement is because Mr Johnson has had a grudge against him following their joint involvement in a previous armed robbery. In either event the jury would be told of Mr Thomas's previous convictions, which he feels would be so overwhelmingly prejudicial to him that the jury might well, in reality, convict him on the basis of that factor alone. He therefore elects to make a statement from the dock setting out his case.

The judge, after directing you upon the law, sums up in the following terms:

'. . . The first witness for the Crown was Mrs White, a young mother who was taking her children to school when all of a sudden she heard the screech of tyres and saw three men, wearing stockings over their faces and armed with what appeared to her to be shotguns, get out of a motor car and attack two security guards who, as we were later to hear when they gave their evidence, were delivering a large sum in cash to the bank. One of these security men attempted to resist one of the robbers and behaved in a way which you may think was of the bravest manner, only to be shot in the leg for his pains. She was unable to identify any of the men involved in the robbery, not surprisingly you may think if they were masked, but was able to give a general description which you have heard. The second witness for the Crown was Mrs Marshal, a pensioner who was on her way to the post office in order to collect her pension. She told you how terrified she was at what she was witnessing, not surprisingly you may think, and later had to have hospital treatment for the shock, Mrs Marshal being a person with a weak heart.'

(The judge carries on dealing in a similar manner with all the other eye witnesses and commending the security men upon their bravery)

'. . . You then heard evidence from Detective Inspector Watson, a police officer with seventeen years' experience in the force. He was the officer responsible for arresting Mr Johnson, a man who, you have heard, pleaded guilty to this offence and who made a full written confession. Now, members of the jury, what Mr Johnson said in the absence of Mr Thomas cannot be evidence against Mr Thomas unless Mr Thomas admits the truth of anything within that statement. The Inspector said that he showed the statement to

Mr Thomas and asked Mr Thomas whether it was true, whereupon Mr Thomas according to the Inspector said yes. The statement of Mr Johnson was read out to Mr Thomas as Mr Thomas was reading it himself and it may assist to remind you of what that statement said.

"All three of us, that is me, Ken and Roger [*Q.* Roger who? *A.* Oh! Roger Thomas] had been planning this blag for some time. We knew that there could be over fifty grand in that van and we all took guns, which Roger had got for us off some geezer in the East end. My gun wasn't loaded, neither was Ken's, the job was heavy enough as it was, only Roger's gun was loaded, I saw him loading it in the car. Well, you know the rest, we arrived at the scene and one of those idiots fancied himself as a hero and had a go. Roger of course had no hesitation in blasting him. . . ."

'Whereupon the inspector asked Mr Thomas quite properly whether what he had just read was true, to which, according to the inspector, he answered yes it was. Now it is a fundamental rule that an admission of guilt voluntarily made by a person is the best evidence available. There has been no suggestion by the defence that such an admission was not voluntary. What the defence say, if you recall, is that it wasn't said at all, and no statement was read to him. The next officer to give evidence was Detective Sergeant Robertson, a man with twelve years' experience in the police force, and who was present at the time of the interview between Mr Thomas and the Inspector, and he corroborates what the Inspector has said. You may think, members of the jury, that if the defence case is to be accepted this officer has got it wrong as well as the inspector. The next officer to give evidence was Detective Constable Smith, the third of the officers who were present at the time of the interview, and he corroborated the evidence given by the inspector and the sergeant. Has he got it wrong as well?

Now in this case the defendant has made a statement to you from the dock in which he denies saying the words alleged by the three police officers and says that he wasn't shown any statements at all. Now a statement which a defendant makes from the dock is not the same as evidence given from the witness box, you will give it such weight as you think fit, but by not giving evidence from the witness box a man cannot be prosecuted for perjury, neither can his statement from the dock be tested by cross examination, and you may think in those circumstances that such a statement carries less weight than sworn evidence. [Had Mr Thomas given the same evidence from the witness box he would have been cross examined on his previous convictions, which the judge would have brought out in his summing up when, by inference, comparing the credibility of his evidence with the evidence of the prosecution witnesses, all people with good character.] Anyway, members of the jury, the issue is entirely one for you but you may think that the major question you have to ask yourself is whether all three police officers have got it wrong in what they have said to you on oath.'

Again apply the same test as with the previous example: assuming that you were perfectly neutral before listening to the judge's summing up, is your state of mind still the same? Or has it been influenced by the nature of the summing up in so far as issues of fact are concerned?

Now compare the above summing up with the following one.

'. . . You have heard a number of eye witnesses give evidence in this case as to the fact that a robbery took place. Their evidence has not been challenged, and it merely goes to prove that there was in fact a robbery, something which is not in dispute. The only issue between the Crown and the defendant is whether or not he was one of those people who were involved in the robbery, and before you can convict Mr Thomas you must be satisfied so that you are sure of his guilt. You have heard what a Mr Johnson, a person who, had he not pleaded guilty, would have been a co-accused in this case, has allegedly said. I must make it quite clear to you that that is not evidence agaist Mr Thomas unless and until Mr Thomas has admitted the truth of it. The Crown's case is that he did admit the truth of it to the police officers, who say they showed him the statement, and when asked whether its contents were true Mr Thomas answered "yes". The real issue then is: are you satisfied so that you are sure that this word was used?

Mr Thomas has not given evidence from the witness box; he has made, as is his right, a statement from the dock. You must not assume guilt merely because a person has not gone into the witness box for there can be many reasons, all consistent with innocence, why this course was adopted. What he has said to you is not evidence in the same sense as sworn evidence, but it is evidence in the sense that you can attach to it such weight as you think fit. In his statement Mr Thomas totally denies using the word yes, and denies being shown a copy of any statement. It is entirely a question for you whether or not this answer was made by Mr Thomas. . . .'

It is, of course, possible to carry on giving numerous examples like the two above, for whatever the charge, whether it be a simple charge of a comparatively minor theft, or a complex fraud or a charge of murder, the issue is always the same – not whether an individual is in fact guilty but whether the summing up of the judge will in many cases influence the minds of one or more members of a jury. The fact that the types of 'summing ups' as given in the above illustrations can and do assert such influence would appear to be beyond question. The fact that summing ups of the type given in the first of either of the above two illustrations regularly occur can easily be ascertained by spending a week in any of the major Crown Court buildings throughout the country and listening to the various summing ups in the various cases without having heard the evidence. In the majority of cases the judge's view of the situation will shine through with the utmost clarity.

It is often thought that the innocent man who has been wrongly convicted will always be able to have his conviction quashed by the Court of Appeal. Regrettably such a proposition will often lie far from reality, for the mere fact that a man is innocent is not a ground of appeal. The reality of the situation in the Court of Appeal is that the court will not interfere with the verdict of the jury unless in *their* view *they* are sufficiently satisfied as to the appellant's innocence, or the trial was so obviously unfair that it suggests that a substantial miscarriage of justice has occurred. They are most unlikely to quash a conviction merely on the basis of the nature of the summing ups which I have provided by way of example. The members of the Court of Appeal are judges who in the overwhelming majority of cases would previously have been barristers. There is little necessity to delve into the complex workings of this particular court for it suffices to say that while it offers some protection to the innocent man wrongly convicted, the reality of the situation is that such protection is often minimal.

Observations and Remedies

There can be few greater wrongs committed against humanity in any free society than the one whereby a judge is allowed to influence members of a jury in reaching their verdict. I reach this conclusion for a number of different reasons, while holding dear the fundamental principle shared by many that it must be totally wrong for an innocent man to be wrongly convicted of a criminal offence.

Firstly, a person who has been arrested, charged and rightly convicted for the offence of murder, for example, cannot do any more harm to society as long as he is safely behind bars. Yet the judge who has, by virtue of his summing up, influenced one member of a jury in reaching a verdict of guilty, is allowed to carry on doing the same thing week after week every time he sits to take a new trial.

Secondly, one of the foundation stones of any free society is the fact that a member of that society can only be branded a criminal in relation to the other members if the other members are satisfied of the individual's guilt after hearing all the evidence and then reflecting upon that evidence without outside influence.

Thirdly, while it is right and proper that a person who occupies the position of a judge, responsible for directing the jury upon the law and seeing that fair play takes place between the opposing parties, is held in the highest esteem in the society which has given to him the powers which he possesses, it becomes a total abuse of those powers if they are used to influence ordinary people in making a decision as to another person's guilt.

Fourthly it is a criminal offence for any defendant to interfere with a member of a jury. The purpose of such interference will be one whereby the defendant hopes the particular juror in question will return a verdict favourable to himself. The offence is called perverting the course of justice and the maximum sentence upon conviction is life imprisonment and/or an unlimited fine. The judge who by virtue of his expertise succeeds in influencing the mind of a juror, resulting in the juror finding a defendant guilty, is not considered to have committed any offence. What is the difference between an individual who, for example, uses some form of threat in order to 'persuade' a juror to return a verdict of not guilty, and a judge who by virtue of his position 'persuades' a juror to return a verdict of guilty?

Every single member of a jury must be free to reach his verdict totally fairly without any pressure or influence being brought to bear by any other person. It can be no defence for a judge, who by the nature of his summing up is able to influence a jury, to state that he does not intend to influence, or that because the nature of his summing up is unlikely to be criticised by another court, he is justified, for a judge well knows the effect his words, or the tone in which he utters them, can have on ordinary people.

It is the height of absurdity that some of England's finest judges sit in the higher civil courts or deal with matters in the High Court when the issue in many cases is one of money, and yet when twelve years of a person's life may be at stake the judge allocated is often one who has not yet achieved such a high status.

The present system for appointing people to the office of a judge is far from satisfactory. Common sense ought to dictate firstly that an individual should never be allowed to take charge of a criminal trial unless he has had a substantial amount of experience in practising at the Criminal Bar, and secondly that such practice should not have been one which was restricted mainly to prosecuting. While politics and the law must always remain separate and distinct, a select committee of members of Parliament from all political parties with at least a few lay members would provide a fairer method of selection than the present system.

Judges, like the majority of other people, ought to be accountable to someone or some body of people for their conduct and behaviour during a trial, and if it is found that the nature of their summing up has brought pressure to bear upon a jury, albeit indirectly, which has resulted in an innocent man being convicted of a criminal offence, this in itself ought to be a wrong for which damages would lie.

CHARACTER

Throughout a trial facts are proved on the basis of evidence, and what evidence can be adduced depends upon the rules of evidence. A detailed analysis or explanation of these rules would belong in another book, but there is one rule of evidence which more than any other could directly contribute to the conviction of an innocent man. This rule is called evidence of character.

Few people who sit on a jury in modern times would allow themselves to become prejudiced against an accused merely because of the type of job which he performs or the fact that he may be unemployed or because of the particular class background he belongs to. However, a man charged with, for example, an offence of armed robbery, could be severely prejudiced in the eyes of one or more members of a jury if they were to be informed that he had previously been convicted of a similar type of offence, however many years ago that might have been. Such a situation, while regrettable, is perhaps in truth a normal facet of human nature, and for that reason our legal system, in common with many others, prevents evidence of a man's previous convictions being adduced during his trial, subject to certain specific exceptions.

The practice of the law tends to make a mockery of this protection, as a result of one of the exceptions to the general rule. This exception, which has already been touched upon earlier, allows evidence of a man's previous convictions to be adduced in evidence at his trial if he goes in the witness box and has cast aspersions upon the character of the prosecution witnesses or has himself, directly or indirectly, given evidence of his own good character. Thus, if an accused suggests that a police officer (for he will be a prosecution witness) is telling lies, that is casting aspersions on the police officer's character in the eyes of the law, and is sufficient to let in evidence of the accused's previous convictions. Similarly, if in a case of rape he were to cast aspersions on the character of the complainant, however true the aspersions were, or to tell the truth and say he is now a hard working family man, this would equally allow evidence of his previous convictions to be adduced.

Another method which will often result in a jury believing that a man has previous convictions has been developed in a far more subtle manner as a result of court practice. When called up for jury service most people will be required to serve on a jury for a period of approximately two weeks. During that time it is usual for jurors to have to serve in a number of different trials, for often a trial may only last for a few days, and as the particular jurors who are chosen for any particular trial will be chosen at random from those jurors who are in the court building, it follows that in many cases at least one or more of the jurors out of the twelve who are eventually chosen will have previously served on a jury, perhaps having just finished one trial. Now after a person has been convicted of a criminal offence, if he has had previous convictions these are read out to the court in the presence of the jury who, although their part is complete, will still be in the jury box and will hear that they have been trying a man with previous convictions. When these jurors go to make up a fresh jury to start a new trial they will often be aware of the rules concerning character, and will have a suspicion that the person whom they are trying is an individual with previous convictions unless they hear to the contrary, for any defence counsel worth his salt when representing a person of good character will have driven this factor home to the jury. If one juror with previous jury experience has not heard of the accused's good character during the trial, he may pass on his suspicions to other members of the jury in the jury room, and the consequences are obvious.

It is not just in the court room that character plays such an important part but in many of the situations which are related to our legal system.

The attitude which one barrister may have towards another

may well depend on the barrister's character. In this context character often means little more than the type of school a person attended or his family background. If two barristers find that they have such matters in common then a different approach to a trial may often follow as opposed to the two barristers who have little in common. Character is also loosely equated with honour in the eyes of many members of the legal profession, and the phrase to 'do the honourable thing' in any given situation may take on a meaning totally foreign to that understood by the ordinary law abiding citizen. I gave an example earlier of how it is considered dishonourable by some barristers for one barrister to ask another for his fees for work which he has performed and for which the other barrister has received payment. Most ordinary people would say that it must be dishonourable for a person to keep money, without just cause, which has been the fruit of another person's labours.

Character also plays its part in the appointment of judges and in the appointment of people to positions in public office. Here it can often mean having kept one's 'nose clean' for a substantial period of time in the sense of not offending others in a superior position to oneself. Character also has to do with educational background as opposed to educational achievement. While it is often easy to justify account being taken of character it is sad that it plays such an overwhelmingly important part, with all its various meanings, in our legal system, often in preference to and at the expense of merit and experience of life.

There can be little doubt that character in all its various forms is part of the basis for class distinction within our society, and a necessary consequence of such distinction will often lead to prejudices and bias, consciously or subconsciously, in one form or another. While it is one thing for class distinction to be socially acceptable it becomes another when it impinges upon the legal system so as to affect an individual's chances of having a fair trial, for then the issues and the dangers involved become of a totally different nature.

FREEDOM OF SPEECH

For the reader, who by now has a much clearer picture of what really occurs in the criminal law branch of the legal system, this chapter provides a necessary compliment to matters which are implicitly involved in the imprisonment of any innocent person.

To suggest to the average law abiding citizen that in England we do not have effective freedom of speech would probably meet with utter disbelief. However, such a person may never, prior to reading this book, have considered the ease with which innocent people can and are imprisoned.

It is necessary to differentiate between freedom of speech and effective freedom of speech. If freedom of speech is given its ordinary meaning as understood by the majority of law abiding citizens, namely the freedom to say what one wants to say or what one believes in without fear of imprisonment or punitive consequences, then subject to the law of defamation and some nearly obsolete exceptions such is the situation which does in fact exist, whereas in many parts of Eastern Europe or the communist countries this is not the case. However, for freedom of speech to have meaning it depends not only upon the content of what one is saying but also upon the person who is saying it. Any person can stand up on a soapbox and state his own personal views, but unless that person has a position of power or authority it is unlikely that what he says will carry much weight or indeed any weight at all, however true it may be. The person who is in a position of power or authority and whose words might carry great weight will often find himself operating under continual restraint caused not by the fear of imprisonment but by the fear of sanctions of no less weight which can easily have the effect of acting upon his mind so as to produce a situation where he is no longer free to say what he feels and believes in and which if said could be of an important public benefit.

History has thrown up numerous examples of the reality of the situation. Politicians have lost their jobs or removed themselves from the running for promotion not necessarily because they have had particular views but because they have dared to voice them in disregard of the party line, or have failed to comply with the commands of the party whips. Lawyers who may have appeared to be 'anti-establishment' in the early part of their careers because of their beliefs soon collect enough black marks against them to prevent or seriously impair their chances of promotion. A lawyer in court who works alternatively for both the prosecution and the defence may soon find his prosecution work tailing off if he is regularly seen when defending to be putting his client's case forcibly, which may regularly involve attacking the prosecuting authorities. Prison governors who hit out at overcrowding in the prisons may soon find the powers that be preventing a further outburst. Top sportsmen are regularly being fined for speaking their minds to the press and the media. The worker dissatisfied with certain of the activities of his trade union may soon find himself out of a job if he publicly discloses too many trade union secrets.

The question has to be asked whether there is really any substantial difference between the situation when a citizen in an Eastern European country speaks out against certain issues and gets locked up for his trouble, and for example a member of parliament in Western Europe who suffers merely because he was publicly seen to stand against the party view on any particular subject. While one type of system may obviously be preferred to the other, does either have true and effective freedom of speech?

The doctrine which acts like a cancer eating away at the principle of freedom of speech is the doctrine of collectivism, whereby a united front must be shown when offering a point of view on any particular topic. There can be little doubt that the existence of this doctrine can be justified in certain exceptional circumstances, national security being one obvious example. Those circumstances apart, whenever the doctrine begins to dominate it does so at the expense of the principle of freedom of speech, and the loss of this principle of necessity involves the withering away of any free society.

To many people, while it is right that an individual should be allowed to state what he believes in, he ought not to be able to destroy the character and reputations of other individuals if that which he is alleging is totally false. It is for this and many other reasons that in England we have the law of Defamation which includes libel and slander. Regrettably, however, while this branch of the law acts to curb abuses of the doctrine of freedom of speech it also acts as a very potent weapon in preventing the justified use of the doctrine. One of the few circumstances in which an individual has no right to legal aid within our system is when he has to defend an action in defamation. It follows, therefore, that however true his words were which caused the action to be brought, he has to find his legal expenses out of his own pocket without any guarantee of being able to recover these if at the end of the day it is proved that one of the defences to the action such as truth or fair comment properly and justifiably exists. The individual with substantial funds can easily bring substantial pressure to bear on another who has made certain allegations against him, however true those allegations may be, which could readily culminate in bankruptcy, for example, particularly when legal costs can readily run into tens of thousands of pounds.

There can be little doubt that effective freedom of speech rarely exists in England. In the legal system only occasionally, when two or more judges have to sit in judgement, will a dissenting opinion be heard, other than in the House of Lords or the Civil Division of the Court of Appeal. The consequences of this situation upon the doctrine of a free society are so obvious as to make further comment unnecessary.

THE JURY AND THE PRESS

It is impossible in a book of this nature which is critical of our legal system to omit mentioning the jury and the press. They are dealt with together because they have one thing in common. The jury are there in a criminal trial to ensure that justice is done, that those who are truly guilty of crimes are convicted, and to prevent the conviction of the innocent. The power of the press acts as a deterrent against abuses of power and against injustice.

No better system has been designed to prevent the conviction of an innocent man than trial by jury, and the continuation of its existence is something which ought never to be disputed. So long as the various members of the jury are chosen at random from ordinary people and no pressure or influence of whatever kind, be it from a judge or any other source, is brought to bear upon them, they will always remain the bulwark of our liberties and the guardians of our freedoms.

If a jury is not truly representative of the people at large a different picture emerges. A jury picked from one particular 'class' of person is likely to draw different inferences from some of the evidence which has been placed before it than a jury containing individuals from different backgrounds and with dissimilar occupations. Equally it can hardly be fair for an individual to stand his trial on a charge of, for example, 'mugging' if the jury is constituted predominantly of young girls under the age of twenty-two or women over the age of fifty-five. Many defence lawyers would agree that on a charge of rape there can be few juries more capable of discerning where the truth lies than one predominantly made up of women over the age of thirty with some experience of life; but can it be right for the average girl under the age of, for example, twenty-two to sit on such a jury?

The preservation of a free press, and by this expression I mean the media generally, goes hand in hand with effective freedom of speech, and is essential to the very existence of a free society. Regrettably, as far as legal matters are concerned, there is sometimes a tendency to dramatise events, but this is more than compensated for by the ability and willingness of the press to expose injustice and to expose any attempt by the legal system to cover up its own inadequacies, particularly when such inadequacies result in a loss of freedom or liberty to the individual.

Unfortunately it is not the reporting of such various items of news which ever poses a real problem but their discovery. A large Crown Court building may consist of up to twenty separate court rooms with trials taking place in each of them, and a reporter cannot be in two places at the same time. Often he might find himself in one court room following a trial which fails to yield the anticipated story, while in the very next court what initially seemed a perfectly innocuous affair is turning into something of great public importance.

The press acts as probably the only real deterrent against the abuse of power by people in authority, for while the doctrine of collectivism will often rear its head in ensuring that policemen, lawyers and judges unite to protect their own, they have little or no control over a free press, the fear of such a force often acting as the ultimate deterrent to more blatant abuses.

MISCELLANEOUS EXAMPLES OF INJUSTICE

Throughout this work every effort has so far been made to avoid giving specific case histories. The reason for this, as was mentioned in the preface, is to prevent the reader getting immersed in a sea of complex legal argument and legal niceties, thus disabling him from seeing a clear picture of what actually occurs within our legal system.

Some of the comments and propositions which have been expounded so far may be so contrary to firmly held and deeply entrenched views that specific case histories will now be provided in order to support the arguments put forward in this work, in the hope that by now the reader will have a much clearer understanding of the criminal law section of the legal system, from the arrest of the citizen until his eventual trial.

Throughout the various actual case histories which I am about to provide the names of the people involved have been changed in order to protect the innocent. Certain irrelevant facts have also been changed in order to prevent identification of the cases, but all the relevant facts which are directly connected with the various propositions contained within this book are exactly as they occurred. Some of the cases are ones in which the writer was directly involved. As to the others, he has made every effort to ensure that the relevant facts as written are true.

Case 1

In the middle of September 1977 an armed robbery took place upon a security van delivering a large sum in cash to a local bank. At least two people were involved in committing the robbery, and at least one of those was armed with a double-barrelled sawn-off shotgun. One of the robbers shot and injured one of the security men.

Eventually one of the people who had been suspected of taking part in the robbery, a Mr White, was interviewed by the police; he was known to be a man with previous criminal convictions and during his interview he admitted his involvement in the actual robbery. This person, notwithstanding the seriousness of the offence, was offered a deal by the police whereby he would be granted immunity from prosecution for the offence if he told the police who had organised the robbery, although the organiser had not been present when the actual robbery had taken place. (It followed, therefore, that all Mr White had to do was 'to come up with a name' in order to retain his liberty.)

Mr White alleged that the organiser was a Mr Brown, a man who Mr White well knew, had an appalling criminal record but who had not been in trouble for some years since his last conviction and appeared to have settled down and been earning an honest living.

Mr Brown was arrested, whereupon not only did he totally deny the alleged offence and denied knowing anything about it but, as a result of his previous experiences with the police, refused to say anything further.

In the meantime the police had arrested another person by the name of Richards who was charged with the offence, and notwithstanding its serious nature, was granted bail, without sureties, by the police. (The situation so far was that the police had arrested two people who they alleged had been involved in the commission of the actual armed robbery. One of those had been granted bail by the police, a most unusual occurrence, while the other had been granted immunity from prosecution. A third person who had nothing to do with the actual robbery was now in custody.)

Mr Brown was subsequently brought up before the Magistrates Court, where he was represented by a barrister, having been granted legal aid, and a strong application for bail was made on his behalf. It was an accepted fact that although he had been in trouble many times before he had never once failed to appear in court to stand his trial, even when he had previously pleaded guilty to offences which he knew in all probability involved an immediate sentence of imprisonment. The police and their lawyer objected to bail on a number of grounds, in particular pointing to the serious nature of the offence, Mr Brown's previous convictions and, because of the substantial sentence of imprisonment which he was likely to receive if he was found guilty, the probability that he would fail to surrender to custody. The magistrates refused Mr Brown bail and he was remanded in custody.

The police did not object to bail in the case of Richards, who was released on unconditional bail and remained on bail right up until the trial.

A number of weeks were to elapse before the prosecution papers which contained the statements made by the various witnesses were served upon the defence, whereupon it became patently obvious that apart from the statement of a person who by his own admission had taken part in the actual robbery there was not a shred of evidence against Mr Brown.

Week after week Mr Brown was brought from prison to the Magistrates Court, numerous bail applications were made on his behalf, which included the offer of substantial sureties and the lack of evidence being clearly pointed out to the magistrates, but each time the answer was the same: bail refused. On one of the occasions the magistrates made his lawyer wait from 10.00am in the morning until 4.00pm in the afternoon before hearing the application for bail. Eventually an application was made to a High Court Judge, which was similarly refused.

After a substantial lapse of time Mr Brown was committed to stand his trial at the Crown Court and then what can only be described as some of the most remarkable events were to occur.

An application for Mr Brown to be admitted to bail was made to the senior judge at the Crown Court where Mr Brown would eventually stand his trial. Substantial sureties were offered and the lack of evidence was pointed out to the judge. The judge refused to hear the sureties, stated that he had not the slightest doubt that Mr Brown would not attend for his trial and dismissed the application, bail refused. Eventually the trial of Brown and Richards was fixed for a specific date, but then the prosecution applied for the trial to be adjourned because, not surprisingly you may think, Mr White had disappeared. It was common ground at the hearing that whatever the reason for Mr White's disappearance it could not in any way be attributed to Mr Brown for he was in prison. Around this time Mr Brown's solicitors received a letter purporting to have been written by Mr White which clearly proclaimed Mr Brown's total innocence of involvement in the whole matter and it later became clear that there were many reasons to account for Mr White's disappearance, none of which were connected in any way with Mr Brown.

By now Mr Brown had spent approximately eight months in prison for an offence which he denied, of which in law he was presumed at that time to be innocent, and for which there existed not a shred of credible evidence. Mr Brown's barrister objected to the prosecution application for the date of the trial to be adjourned because Mr Brown had already spent a substantial time in prison, and because he obviously wanted to be tried and have his innocence proclaimed as speedily as possible. The judge, who was a different judge to the one who had earlier refused Mr Brown's bail application, not only granted the prosecution application, but adjourned the trial for a period of three months with a power to the prosecution to re-apply before the expiry of the three months for a further adjournment, Mr Brown in the meantime being kept in prison. (This posed enormous problems to Mr Brown's lawyers and created a most extraordinary state of affairs, for by this method a man could apparently be denied his trial and kept in prison indefinitely. Mr Brown's lawyers entered into communications with the senior staff of the Divisonal Court of the Queens Bench Division of the High Court, who were of the opinion that the High Court had no jurisdiction in the matter, this being precluded by statute, for the judge's order was one which fell within his discretion as a judge of the court where Mr Brown would eventually be tried. The Court of

Appeal had no jurisdiction because before this court could have jurisdiction there had to be a conviction following a trial upon indictment, and as yet Mr Brown hadn't even been tried let alone convicted.)

Mr Brown's lawyers were then placed in a considerable dilemma as to the next step to take, for it appeared that no other court had jurisdiction in the matter at that time. Application for the old writ of Habeas Corpus appeared out of the question, for having been denied bail it was difficult to see how it could be justifiably argued that Mr Brown was unlawfully in custody and it is a necessary pre-requisite for the issue of the writ to prove that a person's confinement is unlawful.

After a considerable amount of thought Mr Brown's barrister decided to take a most unusual procedural step. He drafted and forwarded a petition to the House of Lords. (Mr Brown's legal aid certificate did not extend to this type of application and as Mr Brown had no money of his own the barrister agreed to undertake the work for the minimum fee that the rules of his profession allowed him to charge, which was approximately £2.) The basis of the content of the petition was that the various actions of the Crown Court which were effectively denying Mr Brown his trial were constitutionally unlawful, even though in England there is no such thing as a written constitution. This action provoked the first piece of positive assistance that Mr Brown was to receive, for the administrative staff of the House of Lords indicated (and one can only presume that there had been consultation upon the matter with at least one Law Lord) that although the Divisional Court may not have jurisdiction to grant a remedy they do have jurisdiction to issue a certificate that a point of law of public importance was involved, and if they were to grant this certificate then this would give the House of Lords jurisdiction in the matter.

Within a very short time of receiving this advice from the Lords one of the most extraordinary of all events was to occur. A summons was received for all the parties in the case, namely solicitors and counsel for the prosecution and the defence, but no witnesses, to appear at the Crown Court of trial. There was no indication as to the purpose of the summons. All parties appeared as requested in response to the summons and the matter was brought before the senior judge (the first Crown Court judge, the reader will recall, who had dismissed Mr Brown's application for bail). The senior judge himself opened the proceedings by wanting to know why Mr Brown was still in custody and made it quite clear that he intended to grant Mr Brown bail. (Whether somebody had had a 'word in the ear' of the judge is something we shall never know.) This sudden change of attitude was something which took Mr Brown's lawyers and Mr Brown completely by surprise, but Mr Brown, and you may think rightly, was far from impressed, for he had been kept in custody for a substantial period of time and it wasn't bail which he now wanted but to be tried. This was made quite clear to the judge, who notwithstanding the prosecution's objections to bail and the refusal of the defence to apply for bail, granted Mr Brown bail on his own volition. (Had Mr Brown been admitted to bail and released from custody it would then have been possible to postpone the trial for a further substantial period of time.) The judge, however, in granting bail, did so on condition that he, Mr Brown, provided a surety or sureties in the sum of two thousand pounds. (Mr Brown had, on his first application for bail to the same judge, which was refused, been able to provide sureties in the sum of ten thousand pounds.) Mr Brown failed to provide the sureties and within a very short time, at long last, Mr Brown stood his trial at the Crown Court before a judge and jury along with Richards, who was alleged to be Mr Brown's co-accused.

At the close of the prosecution case, after they had called all their witnesses, it became patently obvious that there was hardly a shred of evidence to go before the jury, and the trial judge had little choice but to 'throw the case out' and to direct the jury to formally return against Mr Brown a verdict of not guilty, which they duly did. Richards was subsequently convicted and sentenced to two years imprisonment. Mr Brown had served approximately ten months in prison for an offence he had not committed and before he was even allowed to be tried, which taking into account remission of a sentence for good behaviour and the possibility of parole was not far short of the sentence which Richards, who had been found guilty of the offence, was likely to serve.

Mr Brown had no right to any form of compensation.

This case illustrates a number of important propositions which have already been made in this book.

Firstly, a substantial period of the time which Mr Brown spent in prison was spent while he was within the jurisdiction of the Magistrates Court. The overwhelming majority of the applications Mr Brown made for bail were made to this court and again in the overwhelming majority of these applications the magistrates who heard them were people without any legal qualifications. Thus such people were able to deprive Mr Brown, an innocent man, of his liberty for a long period of time without trial.

Secondly, the court instead of acting as a neutral forum for justice was in reality acting as a police court, readily agreeing with the wishes of the prosecuting authority but giving to those wishes the semblance of legal justification, for the police readily gave Richards bail on their own accord and although Richards also had previous convictions, they never raised any objections to such bail continuing. The approach of the police and prosecuting authority in granting Mr White immunity from prosecution was well known to the court but failed to produce any comment or criticism from the court of any kind.

Thirdly, no less than three judges had the opportunity to bring Mr Brown's period of imprisonment effectively to an end, and not one of them was prepared to do so.

Fourthly, the judges of the Crown Court had been able, with comparative ease, to prevent Mr Brown from being tried for as long as they saw fit, without any real remedy being open to Mr Brown.

Fifthly, we see how easy it was for an innocent man, proven to be not guilty of a very serious offence, to be effectively imprisoned for a substantial period of time, not far short of the period which the person who was in fact guilty of the offence spent.

Sixthly, we note the absence of any real right to compensation for Mr Brown for being imprisoned for an offence he did not commit, coupled with the sense of grievance he will undoubtedly have.

Case 2

In October 1979 Mr Anthony Hurst, a young man of nineteen years of age and of previous good character, went along to a discotheque with a few of his friends for an evening's entertainment. During the evening he danced and generally enjoyed himself, leaving at approximately two o'clock in the morning. He left with three girls, one of whom was his fiancée, and a male colleague, all of them being friends of each other. The intention was for Mr Hurst to drop his companions off at their respective homes, all of which were within approximately twenty minutes' drive, whereupon Mr Hurst would then drive home, going to work later that morning.

On the way home, approximately ten minutes after leaving the discotheque, a tragic event occurred. While travelling up a hill Mr Hurst overtook a vehicle being driven by a Mr Moss, and coming in the other direction was another vehicle being driven by a Mr Phillips. An examination of the spot where Mr Hurst overtook showed that it was not the safest spot to have overtaken. After overtaking the vehicle being driven by Mr Moss, Mr Hurst attempted to pull in front of Mr Moss's vehicle in order to avoid the oncoming vehicle being driven by Mr Phillips, but was unable to complete this manoeuvre, for Mr Phillips's vehicle collided with the rear of Mr Hurst's vehicle, which turned over, finally resting upon its roof. Mr Hurst's friend, Mark Smith, who was sitting in the rear of the vehicle, was killed instantly. Mr Hurst received minor injuries but apart from shock no other person was injured.

The police were quickly on the scene. Mr Hurst was not 'breathalysed' but was later interviewed by a number of police officers including a senior inspector who had a great deal of sympathy with all the various parties, including Mr Hurst, who had been involved, and eventually prepared and submitted a report to the relevant prosecuting authorities.

It was eventually decided to charge one person and one person only as a result of the 'accident', and that was Mr Hurst. The charge which was brought against him was the most serious of all the road traffic offences, namely causing death by reckless driving contrary to section 1 of the Road Traffic Act 1972 as amended, an offence which can only be tried upon indictment and one which upon conviction carries a maximum sentence of five years imprisonment.

The magistrates' proceedings were dealt with fairly speedily, due, in no small measure, to the assistance of the police inspector who was in charge of the case and who appeared far from happy with the nature of the charge. He did not object to Mr Hurst being granted bail and Mr Hurst remained on bail right up until his trial.

A period of approximately eight months elapsed from the date of the incident until Mr Hurst was called to stand his trial at one of the most famous court rooms in the world, number one court at the Old Bailey. By this time Mr Hurst could best be described as a bag of nerves, who bore little resemblance to the boy who had innocently gone to the discotheque that evening. He had been unable to work and the case had placed an almost intolerable strain on the whole of his family.

He was represented at his trial by a young and unknown member of the Bar, which was in complete contrast to counsel for the Crown, who was one of the most experienced, capable and efficient junior barristers, an individual who was approximately twice the age of Mr Hurst's counsel. The judge in charge of the trial was a High Court Judge.

Counsel for the Crown when opening his case to the jury made it quite clear that he thought they would have little difficulty in reaching the correct verdict in this case. The Crown would prove that the accused had been driving home with a number of friends, one of which was the dead man, after an evening out at a local discotheque, when he overtook a car on a hill, approaching a bend, at a very excessive speed, with another vehicle travelling in the opposite direction and coming towards him at the same time. The driver of this vehicle took various measures but was unable to avoid the accused's car. A collision occurred, whereupon Mark Smith, a young man who was a passenger in the accused's car, was killed instantly. The Crown would prove that this young man met his death because of the reckless driving of the accused.

The Crown then called their evidence, and after proving that the position where Mr Hurst overtook was far from the safest place to have carried out the manoeuvre – indeed it could readily be inferred that it was a somewhat dangerous place – called as their first eye witness Mr Moss.

Mr Moss was a respectable middle-aged gentleman who was returning home after having been to a card game with his wife when from nowhere he was overtaken by the accused, whose vehicle crossed over to the other side of the road. He assessed the accused's speed as being in the region of 60mph and was adamant that he was travelling very quickly. (Similar evidence was given by Mr Moss's wife, who was a passenger in his car at the time.)

Upon cross examination by counsel for Mr Hurst, Mr Moss agreed that the only way he was able to assess the speed at which Mr Hurst was travelling was by reference to the speed at which his own vehicle was travelling, but he denied that he was travelling particularly slowly. However, defence counsel by further cross examination was able to establish that at the time Mr Moss was in fact travelling in second gear, and the reason for this was that he had just left the home of his friends and that it took a long time for his vehicle, which was a ten-year-old saloon, to warm up.

Mr Phillips was the next witness to give evidence, who stated that the accused's vehicle was travelling very fast because he hadn't seen it until the very last moment and was unable completely to avoid it.

Upon cross examination by counsel for Mr Hurst, Mr Phillips could not be sure whether at the time he was driving with his sidelights on or with dipped headlights. Further cross examination revealed that he was new to the area and at the time of the incident was lost, shortly beforehand having asked his female companion (who did not give evidence) to look at the road map in order to assist with directions. He denied that he may have been glancing at the road map immediately prior to the crash and that he could himself have been guilty of a momentary lapse of concentration which may have accounted for the fact that he had failed to see Mr Hurst's vehicle until the very last moment.

There were various pieces of scientific evidence, none of which was particularly relevant, and that completed the case for the Crown. (Including in the scientific evidence was the evidence of the doctor who had examined the deceased, which proved that the deceased had previously been a healthy man and that death occurred as a result of the crash, an issue not really in dispute.)

The Crown had certainly made out a case fit to go before the jury, and the defence were now placed in a somewhat difficult position for two reasons. Firstly, the only real issue was whether or not Mr Hurst had been driving recklessly, for there could be little doubt that the cause of Mr Smith's death was the crash, and as in many cases the law had defined recklessness as little more than negligence there was evidence at this stage that Mr Hurst had been careless. Secondly, because of the length of time which had elapsed between the crash and the trial Mr Hurst's nerves were in such a state that he was really not fit to give evidence.

Defence counsel decided that although his client would probably incur the wrath of the judge during his summing up to the jury it was only right to advise his client that because of his state of nerves his best interests might lie in making a statement from the dock which Mr Hurst himself would have to write, and give his account of the events to the jury. This would mean that he could not be cross examined by Crown counsel, but then he was not in a fit state to be cross examined. Mr Hurst took his counsel's advice and decided to make a statement to the jury from the dock.

Defence counsel opened his case to the jury and then called upon Mr Hurst to stand up in the dock and say whatever he wished to say to the jury. Mr Hurst told the jury that he had gone to the discotheque where he had met a few friends. During the evening he had generally enjoyed himself but had only consumed one glass of lager. (This was important because although there was no issue of 'drink driving', an inference may well have remained.) The reason why he had only had such a small amount to drink was because most of the time he had been dancing. He recalled travelling behind another vehicle which was travelling very slowly, and having remained behind this vehicle for approximately two minutes he pulled out to overtake. He did not notice anything coming the other way. As he was overtaking he suddenly became aware of the oncoming vehicle and was trying to pull in when the crash occurred. He was unable to remember anything else of the incident. (Although this was the substance of his evidence, the manner in which he gave it not surprisingly left a lot to be desired.) Mr Hurst then sat down.

The next defence witness was a young lady who had been a passenger in the defendant's car. She corroborated the fact that Mr Hurst had drunk very little that evening and that he had spent most of his time on the dance floor. She couldn't remember anything about the incident. She did not notice anything about the speed at which she was travelling but she would not have called it fast. Upon cross examination by counsel for the Crown she admitted that she was the defendant's fiancée. That concluded the case for the defence.

Counsel for the Crown then made his closing speech to the jury, reminding them of the meaning of 'recklessness', which he equated nearly but not quite with negligence. He pointed out the similarities between negligence and carelessness, and then reminded the jury of the stretch of road where the crash took place, and in particular of the evidence of Mr Moss. He commented that on the evidence the jury could be satisfied so that they were sure that the defendant's driving at that particular time was reckless.

Counsel for the defence then made his closing speech to the jury and approached the situation in a different manner. The whole situation was a tragic sequence of events culminating in the death of the defendant's friend. However much one might like to, nothing could bring this young man back to life. True Mr Hurst had been guilty of something, but on the evidence that was at the most an error of judgement, and by no reasonable stretch of the imagination could his driving be described as reckless.

The judge then summed up to the jury, having first directed them upon the law in terms very similar to those adopted by counsel for the Crown. He reminded them of the evidence of Mr Moss and Mr Phillips. At no stage did he mention the defence point of 'error of judgement', and there could have been little doubt that the view he himself adopted was in many ways similar to the view adopted by the Crown as opposed to the defence.

The jury then retired to consider their verdict and after approximately forty five minutes came back with a note for the judge which requested further guidance on the meaning of negligence. The judge directed them in terms similar to those mentioned by counsel for the Crown in his closing speech, and the jury again retired. Fifteen minutes later the jury again returned with a further note which asked, in effect, whether if they found that the defendant was guilty of an error of judgement he would be guilty of the offence. The judge, with a look which appeared to be one of surprise on his face, was bound to give them an answer in the negative and he duly did.

A period of approximately two hours was to elapse before the jury returned for the last time to announce that they had reached their verdict. The procedure went as follows: the clerk to the court requested the foreman to stand and asked him the following questions, receiving the answers as stated.

'Members of the jury, have you reached a verdict upon which you are all agreed?'
The foreman replied, 'Yes.'
'Do you find the defendant, Anthony Hurst, guilty or not guilty of causing death by reckless driving?'
The foreman replied, 'Not guilty'.
'And is that the verdict of you all?'
The foreman replied, 'Yes it is'.

Mr Hurst left that most famous court room in a pitiful state, his ordeal over, but a different young man from the one who many months earlier had ventured out for a normal social evening.

This case illustrates a number of points but perhaps one of the most relevant for the purposes of this book is the damage which can so easily be caused by having the fact of a trial hanging over a person's head for any length of time. It could not be doubted that there was a case for Mr Hurst to answer, but equally there was little doubt that a jury made up of ordinary people would be loath to convict of such a serious offence on the circumstances of the case, for the situation was tragic rather than criminal. Yet the prosecuting authorities, although they have a considerable amount of discretion as to whether to bring such proceedings in the first place or having brought them whether to continue them, had little hesitation in prosecuting. This is in total contrast to the situation when, for example, an individual loses his life as a result of conduct by the police or by other people who may be in positions of authority, for in such circumstances every effort is made to prevent a trial of the matter unless there is strong evidence of guilt.

Those responsible for continuing the prosecution against Mr Hurst were totally unable to see the human angle involved in the case, being content to apply strictly legalistic reasoning. Such a situation can easily occur whenever those who are in positions of power automatically treat the word 'emotion' as being something which has no place in a legal system, when in reality in all its various meanings it can at the proper time be one of the most important of human attributes.

One can only hope that since the above events Mr Hurst has been able to pick up the threads of his life again, and is able to put to the back of his mind the sequence of those tragic events which will undoubtedly haunt him for many years to come.

Case 3

The facts of this case are as follows: Robert Adair was a young man who came from a very modest background and who eventually decided that his future lay in the field of law. He was a strong believer in the English legal system and in justice generally, such basic beliefs being taught to him ever since he was a small boy. His parents, however, had insufficient money to send him to college for higher education, and he was not a person to take money from the state if he could avoid it.

One day Mr Adair bought a large, older-style, semi-detached property, borrowing the majority of the money he required for the purchase and giving to the lender the security of a mortgage over the property. He moved into the property, living in it as his home, and slowly converted most of it into a number of bedsitting rooms which he intended to utilise in order to bring him in an income, and started studying at night school for a law degree, the fees for his studies being met from his own resources. He shortly got married, he and his wife living in part of the house, a number of lodgers living in the remainder and paying a weekly sum.

Mr Adair soon became aware of the provisions of various Acts of Parliament generally referred to as the Rent Acts. To the average reader these Statutes would probably simply be provisions designed to prevent the unscrupulous landlord from charging an exorbitant rent and then using force in order to evict tenants on to the streets who could not afford to pay. However, Mr Adair soon observed that apart from the general policy of the Act, for which it could be argued there was justification, enacted within the main body of the Statute was, as many law students know, a piece of legislation based upon a pure theoretical doctrine of Karl Marx; for the Act made it possible for an individual living in somebody else's home to refuse to pay any rent and be protected from eviction for a substantial period of time, thus having the effect of depriving a person of his own home for periods of time without giving any right to compensation.

In order to try and avoid the above situation from occurring Mr Adair drew up a series of simple agreements which he required prospective lodgers to enter into before he would allow them into his home. These agreements had the effect, if valid, of preventing a person who refused to pay rent or otherwise caused a nuisance from remaining in Mr Adair's home for any substantial period of time. Mr Adair made clear to all prospective occupants not only the meaning behind the agreements but also the reasons for the agreements in the first place. The purpose of the agreements was not to deal with questions of whether the rent was fair or unfair, but simply to prevent people from staying in his home without paying any rent, or who caused a nuisance to others. For a period of time everything ran comparatively smoothly. Various different types of people came and went, staying in the house for various periods of time, and none of them complained about the agreements into which they entered.

Mr Adair's income after paying all expenses was however still far too small to enable him to maintain anything other than the barest standard of living. Consequently he took a part-time job in order to supplement this income, all the time continuing his studies. His marriage started to go through a difficult period which was eventually to lead to a divorce.

One day, following an advertisement in the local paper, a young man by the name of David Horseman applied for one of the rooms. He informed Mr Adair of his occupation and signed the various agreements, leaving Mr Adair a deposit of £20, which was to be returned to Mr Horseman when he left providing he had stayed for at least six months and had given two weeks notice.

During the time that Mr Horseman was in occupation of the room Mr Adair became increasingly concerned by various odours which appeared to emanate from Mr Horseman's room, and which resembled the odour of inflammable liquids or substances which are used in photography, but no evidence was ever obtained. However, the relationship between Mr Horseman and Mr Adair became somewhat strained. One day after Mr Horseman had been in occupation of his room for a period of approximately six weeks, Mr Adair gave to him his apportionment of the electricity bill. Mr Horseman refused to pay any part of it. Heated discussions took place, whereupon Mr Horseman made various threats to Mr Adair, finally stating that he would leave the premises, refused to pay any proportion of the electricity bill and insisted upon having his full deposit of £20 returned. Mr Adair had no intention of giving Mr Horseman his deposit back because taking into account the cost of re-advertising and the cost of electricity Mr Horseman would have been in occupation of the room for a nominal amount. Mr Adair could even have lost money on the transaction taking into account how long he might have to wait to obtain a suitable client for Mr Horseman's room. However, because of the threats, Mr Adair agreed to return Mr Horseman's £20 if he called the following Friday. During the period which Mr Horseman spent in Mr Adair's home he had got on friendly terms with another young man who was staying in the house, a Mr Stuart Thomson, a person who, so far, had not caused Mr Adair the slightest trouble.

Mr Horseman left Mr Adair's home on the Tuesday, two days after the argument had taken place, moving into new accommodation. He had taken with him all his own personal property and possessions from the room which he had occupied, except for a pillow slip. He called back on the Friday to collect his £20, having unbeknown to Mr Adair one hour earlier been to the local Rent Tribunal.

When Mr Horseman arrived at Mr Adair's home he was with another individual who was unknown to Mr Adair and who, Mr Adair alleged, was approximately six feet tall, dressed in a 'donkey' jacket and jeans, and who gave the impression that he had been called upon by Mr Horseman to 'assist' him in collecting the money. This was subsequently to be denied by Mr Horseman. Instead of receiving the £20 Mr Horseman was served with a summons claiming damages off Mr Horseman for breach of the initial agreement and for non-payment of the electricity account.

What was now to occur was a most remarkable series of events which were to spread over many years. Within a very short time of Mr Horseman's departure Mr Adair received a communication written in official language from the local Rent Tribunal which informed Mr Adair that they intended to visit the house and inspect the room occupied by Mr Horseman. Mr Adair wrote back informing them that Mr Horseman had left the premises and did not consider that they had any jurisdiction in the matter. Various heated correspondence was then exchanged culminating in the Tribunal demanding entry and suggesting that Mr Adair was guilty of a criminal offence. Mr Adair replied by denying them a right of entry, asserting that any such entry would be a Trespass and consequently it would be they and not he who would be committing the wrong, and if they did enter he would eject them from the land. Mr Adair's correspondence for all practical purposes was to fall on deaf ears, and finally the Tribunal informed Mr Adair of the date and time when they were going to enter the land. (The following account of what took place when the Tribunal entered upon Mr Adair's land is for the sake of coherency a mixture of the neutral facts and part of the evidence which was later to be disputed. The reader will be able to form his own conclusions in due course.)

The members of the Tribunal came to Mr Adair's home at the time and on the day that they had previously threatened. A few hours earlier Mr Adair had locked and secured all the external doors to his home and securely tied with string the front gate which led into the path up to the front door. On arrival, the members of the Tribunal had no hesitation in forcing open the front gate. They then walked up the path and continuously rang the front doorbell immediately adjacent to the glass front door. Eventually Mr Adair, who was in the house at the time, could tolerate the ringing no longer and turned off the electricity supply which fed the doorbell, whereupon for a substantial period of time the members of the Tribunal banged and hammered upon both the wood and glass parts of the front door. They did not receive entry and eventually left the premises. Mr Adair was left in what he was later to describe as a state of shock, for although only minor damage had been caused to the property and Mr Adair could not be described as a physically weak person, the people who had entered upon his land in defiance of his prohibition were not ordinary people, or debt collectors, or even policemen, but were people who were in a position equivalent to that of a judge, and the wrong which they had perpetrated was against a law student, who could not possibly believe that such conduct could occur.

Various protracted correspondence then took place between Mr Adair and the Tribunal, who appeared to have been somewhat incensed at having been denied access to Mr Adair's home. All this was having an adverse effect upon Mr Adair's studies, and eventually Mr Adair informed the Tribunal that notwithstanding the very serious view he personally took of the situation, coupled with the fact that there could be little doubt that they had broken the law, so far as he was concerned he was prepared to accept a nominal amount of damages providing they made a full apology accepting the fact that they were wrong. Mr Adair received neither his nominal damages nor any apology, but instead the Tribunal maintained that they were in the right and it was Mr Adair who was in the wrong.

Mr Adair took the view that there was little point in studying law if he was merely to allow the situation to pass, particularly as there was nothing whatsoever to prevent these so-called 'judges' from committing the same acts over and over again. Accordingly, as they consistently refused to accept that they were in the wrong, Mr Adair commenced legal proceedings against the Tribunal, which initially were for a Court of law to decide who was right but which developed into an action for Trespass to Mr Adair's land and for which Mr Adair claimed damages and exemplary damages. (The reader ought to be aware that general damages are intended to compensate for any loss actually suffered which in this case would probably extend to any damage caused to the front gate or to the front door which would only be a nominal amount; exemplary damages, on the other hand, are not meant to compensate at all but are meant to punish the wrongdoer, particularly when any general damages which may be awarded would be totally inadequate bearing in mind the nature of the wrong which had been perpetrated. Such damages can only be awarded in certain exceptional cases, one of those being when there has been an abuse of power by servants of the Government, police officers and similar classes of persons acting in a position of authority.)

Mr Adair, although still merely a law student, personally prepared all the paperwork involved in putting his case. These, perhaps not unnaturally, left a lot to be desired but he certainly could not afford proper legal representation and in any event his intrinsic belief in the legal system was such that as far as he was concerned all he had to do was to go into the witness box and tell the truth. During one of the various preliminary applications, which took place before a very senior High Court Judge, Mr Adair made an application for the trial of the issue to take place before a jury. This application was refused and was also opposed by the Tribunal. Perhaps after being refused a jury warning bells ought to have started ringing loud and clear in Mr Adair's ears, but he still diligently plodded on, for after all could he fail to receive justice at the hands of a High Court judge?

It took quite a few years for the matter eventually to come for trial, during which time Mr Adair had passed his law degree. Only approximately two months earlier he had achieved his ambition and been called to the Bar. When the matter came for trial the action against Mr Horseman was joined with the action against the Tribunal so that both matters could be heard and dealt with at the same time. The judge was a senior

judge of the Chancery Division who was sitting as a High
Court Judge and who was also a Queens Counsel.

Mr Adair, as the Plaintiff, stood up to open his case to the
judge, whereupon as the record clearly shows he was met with
a barrage of cross examination by the judge, which of course
prevented him from opening his case in his own way, and the
next step which almost immediately followed was for Mr Adair
to go into the witness box.

Mr Adair gave evidence of the agreement with Mr Horseman
when Mr Horseman first came to his home to view the room.
He stated to the judge that the reasons for the agreement were
to prevent the situation in which a person could refuse to
honour his obligations, could cause a nuisance to other
members of the house, and could yet be immune from eviction
for a substantial period of time. He stated how this had all
been clearly explained to Mr Horseman, who had earlier told
him that he was an industrial chemist. He went on to describe
how Mr Horseman had not paid anything towards his electricity bill and how he had agreed to return to Mr Horseman his
£20, notwithstanding that he had only been in occupation for
a very short period of time and had left without giving any
real notice, because he had been threatened by Mr Horseman
that if he didn't give him the money Mr Horseman would go
to the Rent Tribunal. Mr Horseman also enquired as to
whether Mr Adair paid income tax and made various other
implied threats connected with the furniture in the room
which Mr Horseman had occupied. Mr Adair then told how
Mr Horseman had vacated the room on the Tuesday, two days
after the argument concerning the electricity bill, and had
removed all his personal belongings, and how Mr Horseman
had arrived on the Friday in order to collect the £20. He stated
that when Mr Horseman arrived he was not alone but was
accompanied by a person whom he had never seen before, and
he went on to describe this person as an individual approximately six feet tall, well built, dressed in a donkey jacket and
jeans, who gave the impression that he was there to assist Mr
Horseman in getting the £20. He subsequently gave evidence
as to the various correspondence which had been entered into
with the Tribunal and was able to point to agreed documentary
evidence which clearly and unequivocally showed the prohibi-

tion from entering upon his land and what was likely to occur if they did enter, and how this prohibition had been totally ignored. He then went on to describe how, on the day the Tribunal did enter, he had previously securely tied the front gate and had checked it very shortly before the time when they were due to arrive. He related how the Members of the Tribunal arrived, forced open the front gate, and then for a prolonged period of time rang the front door bell. Mr Adair having turned off the electricity supply which fed the bell, these men had then proceeded to hammer and bang upon the front door for a substantial period of time. He stated why he was extremely frightened at the time, not because of any damage which was caused to the property, which he admitted was nominal, but because of the type of people who were causing the damage, for at that time he was a law student and the people who were committing the wrong were people who to him were in the same position as judges. (The judge agreed that they were judges in a sense and this as the reader will see was probably one of the few relevant factors with which the judge did agree!)

Both Mr Horseman, who was legally aided, and the Tribunal had the benefit of being represented by solicitor and counsel, and Mr Adair was then subjected to cross examination by both counsel, but he did not budge from his evidence. Of far more significance, however, he was also subjected to cross examination by the judge who, unbeknown to Mr Adair, had used his authority in order to obtain from court records confidential details of Mr Adair's divorce! Mr Adair's ordeal in the witness box lasted nearly three days, but even at the end of this period the judge had not yet finished with him, for he then called for the details connected with Mr Adair being called to the Bar, and Mr Adair had little doubt of the true purpose that lay behind these questions.

Mr Horseman then gave evidence. He stated that when he first went to Mr Adair's home he was a student though he had since qualified as an industrial chemist. (Mr Adair had rarely taken in students and it is difficult to understand why he should make an exception in Mr Horseman's case let alone lie about it.) He had signed the various agreements but did not understand them. He denied that he had threatened Mr Adair but agreed that he had mentioned the Corporation and the Tribunal to Mr Adair. (It would have been difficult for him to have denied these facts for there was clear documentary evidence.) When he called to collect the £20 he was not with any tall stranger as described by Mr Adair but was with Mr Thomson; which Mr Thomson was later to corroborate. (This was something which took Mr Adair completely by surprise. The reader ought to be aware that in civil proceedings, unlike criminal proceedings, both parties know before the trial any matters which are in dispute. At no stage until now had Mr Horseman or his solicitors informed Mr Adair that this suggestion was going to be made, although Mr Horseman's solicitors well knew the allegation which Mr Adair was making.)

Mr Horseman and Mr Thomson were then subjected to a small amount of cross examination by Mr Adair with the judge playing his part in interrupting Mr Adair.

The members of the Tribunal were then to give evidence, one of them before doing so entering into a prolonged discussion with the judge about matters concerning his military service. They agreed that they arrived at Mr Adair's home with the intention of entering and agreed that they had received the various notices prohibiting them from entering the property or any of the land. They denied forcing the gate or breaking the string. (This was notwithstanding that they had previously made written admissions which tended to prove the contrary.) They could not recall any extensive banging upon the front door.

By the time it came to cross examine the witnesses for the Tribunal, the attitude of the judge and the pressure which he had brought to bear, coupled with the nature of the questions which he had asked Mr Adair regarding his recent calling, and which could only have had one objective, had undoubtedly taken their toll. Mr Adair hardly cross-examined one of the witnesses and did not bother asking any questions at all of the other. He further refused to make a closing speech to the judge and only when the judge virtually insisted did he do so.

The judgement delivered by the judge was a complete and total character assassination of Mr Adair. He was however 'driven' to find that the Tribunal had trespassed (he could hardly do anything else for there was irrefutable documentary evidence of this fact) but suggested that such a Trespass was of the most trivial nature. He awarded to Mr Adair one half penny in damages. He dismissed Mr Adair's claim against Mr Horseman and ordered him to pay to Mr Horseman £20. (Mr Horseman, therefore, did not even have to pay towards the electricity which he had used.) He further ordered Mr Adair to pay the full costs of the proceedings, which amounted to a sum of approximately seven thousand pounds.

Although the trial had come to an end there was to be a most extraordinary sequel to the case. Mr Adair's suspicions of the purpose behind the judge's questions to him were shortly to be confirmed, for the judge had written a letter, which was dated *before* the end of the trial, to the disciplinary body of the Senate of the Inns of Court, the body responsible for disciplinary proceedings against a barrister. The letter contained a number of very serious allegations against Mr Adair made by the judge, and these included allegations which in reality amounted to perjury and malicious prosecution against the Tribunal. The contents of this letter, as the judge well knew, could easily have led to Mr Adair being disbarred.

After the trial Mr Adair had to pick up the threads of the career which he had only just started. He had managed to obtain a pupillage in what was reputed to be a very 'good' set of chambers and it was after he had completed his pupillage that the shock was to occur. A bundle of documents arrived at the chambers from the Senate containing details of the charges which Mr Adair was going to be required to defend, but even now when the profession for which he had worked so hard to achieve was at stake, he was not to be allowed a jury any more than he had been allowed a jury at his trial.

Within a matter of days of his having received the papers from the Senate he was told to leave his chambers, although no mention was made to him of the disciplinary proceedings and the official reason given to him was merely that his pupillage had come to an end. He therefore found himself without a set of chambers from which he could continue the small practice which he had started to develop.

A period of over two years was to elapse between the date of the judge's letter and the disciplinary hearing against Mr Adair and the delay was not attributable to Mr Adair. Mr

Adair was represented by counsel, the Senate who were bringing the proceedings also being represented by counsel. The hearing was essentially held in private, apart from the presence of certain individuals who were necessary to the proceedings. The Tribunal which was to decide the matter was presided over by a High Court Judge (the reader will recall that the complaint originated from a person who had been sitting in the capacity of a High Court Judge) with a number of members of the Bar and a small minority of lay members. Essentially the Senate were judge, jury and prosecuting authority all rolled into one. Mr Adair has no complaints about the fairness of the hearing if in such circumstances a hearing could ever be fair without a jury. Eventually the Tribunal, having heard the evidence (the judge was not called upon to give evidence), found some of the charges proved and some not proved. Which charges were found to be proved and which were not is not really relevant, for it suffices to say that the Tribunal did not call upon Mr Adair's counsel to mitigate, indicating that in their view they did not feel that the charges which they found to be proved merited anything other than a reprimand, one of the most minor forms of sentences which the Senate with their substantial powers could make. There was not one word of criticism directed against the judge.

Mr Adair then decided to appeal against this decision, and in order to do so had to serve various notices on various people, which he duly did, and to comply with certain strict time limits. However, in order to draft the grounds of his appeal properly he required a copy of the transcript of the proceedings which had taken place before the Tribunal and this he duly requested. However, it soon became obvious that, not unusually, he was not going to receive the transcript within the required time, and in such circumstances he was obliged to apply to the Lord Chancellor for an extension of the time. This he duly did and the Lord Chancellor refused his application. He then wrote to the Lord Chancellor asking him for his reasons for refusing what appeared such a simple request. The Lord Chancellor replied saying that he was not obliged to give reasons.

Mr Adair is now trying to develop his practice in the far

north of England, many hundreds of miles away from the scene which was to cause such untold suffering.

General Observations

There are many observations which can be made as a result of this case, a number of which the reader will already be aware of. Where the truth lay of the various issues between Mr Adair, Mr Horseman and the Tribunal is a matter which must now rest with the reader, who may not have much difficulty in resolving it. Certain features of the case were of particular relevance.

Firstly, the Statute which created the problem in that it sought to deprive people of their own homes for various substantial periods of time without compensation has, in so far as these provisions are concerned, its roots firmly entrenched in the doctrines of the philosophy of Marx and Engels, two philosophers who have usually tended to play a part in the legislative process of Eastern European Countries as opposed to our own system. The various methods of enforcement which are given by Parliament to the Tribunal, again in so far as these particular provisions are concerned, require a process which is inquisitorial. Suffice it to say that this process is also one which is used in Eastern European Countries.

Secondly, Mr Horseman finished the case without being out of pocket and without having had to pay anything towards the cost incurred by Mr Adair for the electricity which he used while in Mr Adair's home.

Thirdly, on the main issue between Mr Adair and the Tribunal, namely the issue of Trespass, Mr Adair was proved right. However, for bringing the action, although it is difficult to see what else he could have done in the circumstances, he was effectively 'fined' many thousands of pounds by having to pay the other parties' costs. It must therefore follow that in such circumstances an individual ought not to bring an action before the courts for the determination of his rights in his own land when such rights have been challenged by others in authority.

Fourthly, the value which this judge placed upon the deliberate violation of Mr Adair's land by those in a position of power was one halfpenny. The reader must ask himself what value he places upon such a principle in connection with his own land.

Fifthly, although theoretically the disciplinary proceedings which were brought against Mr Adair were brought as a result of what took place at the trial, by which time Mr Adair was a qualified barrister, the reality of the situation was that he was effectively to be 'branded' forever for bringing the proceedings in the first place which he had commenced many years prior to having attained any legal qualifications whatsoever.

Sixthly, the particular judge who sat as the trial judge is allowed to carry on sitting in judgement against others who may wish to bring proceedings of a similar nature against those in authority.

Seventhly, Mr Adair had been deprived of a jury at the trial notwithstanding that the issue was one between an individual and those in positions of authority.

Eighthly, Mr Adair had no right to a jury made up of members of the public when the decision was to be made as to whether he was a fit and proper person to represent, or to continue representing, other members of the public.

It must follow from what has just been stated that many of the matters which were raised earlier in the chapters on judges and barristers are now clearly illustrated. It would appear, and it is most regrettable, that certain judges are not prepared to accept that when they occupy their positions they do so as servants of the public not as their masters. The 'judges' who trespassed upon Mr Adair's land are for all practical purposes immune from action. The judge who presided at the trial was allowed to wreak havoc not only at the trial itself, by adopting many techniques including the use of character assassination based on wholly irrelevant material including confidential divorce papers, but also after it, when providing his 'information' to the disciplinary body. In both instances he was immune from any action. The laws of England will never be able to control flagrant abuses of power such as took place in this case unless those in authority are prepared to enforce them.

As has been already mentioned, the trial judge is still sitting in judgement upon others, and the question which the reader must answer himself is simply this. Would you consider that you are likely to receive a fair trial if that particular judge was to sit in judgement upon yourself, your children or any members of your family?

Case 4

One evening at approximately 11.00pm a fight broke out in a public house which resulted in one man being injured and two men being charged with a serious offence of assault.

The two accused were eventually brought before the Magistrates Court during which a bail application was made on their behalf, which was opposed by the police and which resulted in bail being refused. A few weeks later certain items of evidence came into the possession of the defence lawyers which tended to illustrate the weakness of the prosecution case and, coupled with various other new factors, justified the decision to make another bail application on behalf of the two accused men, who so far had protested their innocence.

Solicitors for the accused instructed counsel to make the application for bail, and he duly attended the Magistrates Court, arriving before 10.00am. The officer in charge of the case recognised and accepted that there had been a change in circumstances since the last application for bail had been made though he indicated to the defence lawyer that he still intended to oppose the application for bail, leaving it to the court to decide the issue after the usual argument.

A few minutes before 1.00pm the case was called on. Counsel for the accused explained the fact that he wished to make an application for bail and that there were new factors which had come to light since the last application for bail had been made many weeks earlier.

The magistrates refused to hear the bail application at all and also refused to hear the facts, which amounted to a change in circumstances, and remanded the accused in prison for a further seven days.

Some time after, in a totally different Magistrates Court, an individual was charged with an offence in relation to cannabis resin, a controlled drug. He was represented by counsel who had been instructed to make a bail application on his behalf. The police officer objected to bail but the objections which he gave to the court were insufficient to deny bail according to the Statutory provisions. The clerk to the court then 'assisted' the police officer in formulating his objections. The magistrates did not retire in order to consider their decision but took approximately a matter of a minute to refuse bail. The reasons which they gave were again inadequate according to the Statutory provisions, and again the clerk to the court assisted them, having previously misdirected them on a question of law.

Both the above cases were later to be heard by a Divisional Court of the Queens Bench Division of the High Court. Four different High Court Judges were to hear the facts of the above cases. Both applications to the High Court were for the issue of the writ of Habeas Corpus to release the various defendants from custody. (The success of these applications would not have meant that the accused would be free and would not have to stand their trial; its effect would merely have been that they would not have been in prison while awaiting trial.)

In both cases the grounds of the application to the High Court were somewhat complex but in substance were similar, for the essence of the applications was simple, namely that as the magistrates had failed to comply with the provisions of an Act of Parliament which gave a right to bail (in the first case they had not even bothered to hear the application for bail at all) the fact that they had then remanded the defendants into custody without complying with the law must necessarily mean that such confinement to prison was unlawful.

The Divisional Court refused both applications for the issue of the writ of Habeas Corpus. The complexities of the legal arguments are not relevant to this work save to say that the practical effect of these decisions is that magistrates do not have to comply with the rules of evidence when deciding whether to keep a man imprisoned before trial, may totally ignore the provisions of an Act of Parliament, namely the Bail Act 1968, before remanding a person to prison, and, however wrongful their actions may be, the individual who has been imprisoned as a result of those actions is not in prison unlawfully. His only remedy is the 'secret' remedy of making a fresh application for bail to a judge sitting in chambers.

These cases clearly illustrate how an individual charged with a criminal offence in a number of instances can find himself with less rights, so far as his liberty is concerned, before trial and when he is presumed to be innocent, than he will have during his trial or even after he has been convicted. Before a person can be imprisoned for a criminal offence a necessary prerequisite is that a jury will have found him guilty of that offence. A jury will only find him guilty in accordance with the evidence and such evidence which can be adduced against him is dependent upon the rules of evidence. However, for the magistrates to deprive him of his liberty before his trial, they do not have to comply with the rules of evidence at all. After a person has been found guilty of a criminal offence, if the judge has made a substantial error of law the convicted person can apply to the Court of Appeal in order to have his conviction quashed. Rarely will the Court of Appeal in such circumstances order a new trial, but before trial the magistrates appear to be able to make as many errors of law as may occur, and the only remedy for the unfortunate accused is to have the matter re-heard before a judge.

Case 5

In the middle of January 1980 a number of offences of armed robbery took place in the Kent area. All the robberies were committed on the same day and within a very short distance of each other.

In the first robbery two young men, one coloured and one white, one of whom was armed with a double-barrelled shotgun sawn off approximately twelve inches from the trigger, entered a jeweller's shop and robbed the jeweller of cash and certain items of jewellery.

The second robbery took place approximately forty-five minutes later when two youths, one coloured and one white, robbed the owner of a small grocery shop of approximately sixty pounds in cash. No weapons were fired.

The third robbery took place one hour after the second and

within a distance of one mile from the scene of the second robbery. The proprietor of an off-licence had just finished neatly stacking a large number of cans of orange drink when two young men, one coloured and one white, entered the shop. The white man was armed with a double-barrelled sawn-off shotgun. The coloured man threatened the shopkeeper with force unless he handed over the contents of the till. The shopkeeper, not unnaturally, succumbed to the threats, and during the robbery the white man discharged the shotgun at the pyramid of orange cans which all came cascading down from the counter.

The fourth and fifth robberies took place in a similar style on two local shops within a few hundred yards of each other and within a mile of where the third robbery had taken place. On both occasions money was stolen but no gun was fired.

The sixth, and what was to be the last robbery on that day within the particular area took place on a garage. In this robbery the cashier at the garage was threatened with a knife by one of two young men, one coloured and one white, whereupon she handed over the money which was in the till.

In none of the robberies was anybody injured, and following the last robbery a motor car was chased by a number of police vehicles. Eventually the vehicle turned into an industrial estate, and the occupants decamped. Within a matter of minutes the police vehicles which had been in pursuit arrived, only to find the vehicle which they had been chasing abandoned. A quick search of the vehicle immediately yielded a double-barrelled sawn-off shotgun, found under the rear seat. In the glove compartment and in other parts of the vehicle various items were discovered which had been stolen during the various robberies which had taken place that day.

A thorough search of the area took place and within one hour of its commencement two men, one coloured and one white, were arrested. Approximately five hours later a white youth was found on the roof of one of the buildings in the vicinity of where the motor vehicle had been abandoned. This youth was arrested and taken into custody. None of the three people arrested provided any resistance to the police, and the first two who had been arrested made certain admissions consistent with guilt and with their involvement in the robberies.

The youth who had been arrested on the roof of the building did not make any admissions of any kind, and was later described by the arresting officer as having been found in a dazed state. He was taken to the police station and interviewed, when again he made no admissions of guilt. All his clothing, except his underpants, was removed from him, and he was locked in a cell covered only in a blanket where he was to remain for a period of approximately twelve hours. This boy was fifteen years of age. The other two, who had been arrested first, were nineteen and twenty-eight years of age. The boy was not allowed to see his parents and approximately fourteen hours after his arrest he was interrogated by the senior police officer in charge of the case in the presence of a social worker who was unknown to the boy and who had been called in by the police. He was alleged to have made a full confession of guilt which was allegedly written down by the police officer at the boy's dictation. This boy could not read or write.

The matter was eventually to come for trial before the Crown Court. The first two men who had been arrested pleaded guilty to the various offences of robbery, the coloured boy on the basis that he was one of the young men who took part in the robberies, and the white man on the basis that he was driving the car, which was later found abandoned, and which was used to drive the other two to the various premises which were robbed. Only the fifteen-year-old boy pleaded not guilty, and he alone was to be tried for six offences of armed robbery, all of which were to be tried together before a jury.

The boy's instructions to his lawyers, which were to provide the basis for his defence, were very simple, and yet because they were so simple they were to produce a highly complex situation. His defence was that he was unemployed with few friends, one of whom was the coloured youth. On the morning of the day when the robberies took place he had met the coloured boy and was given two pills and a quantity of whisky. He was unable to say what these pills were. He recalled getting into the vehicle which was used in all the robberies but then was unable to remember anything else until he found himself in a cell in the police station. In so far as his 'confession' was concerned, the policeman was virtually telling him what to say by describing the events which had occurred. It followed from what the boy had informed his lawyers that the prosecution had to be put to proof that the boy had committed the robberies, although in reality there was probably little doubt, but the real issue was the state of the boy's mind at the time.

The first matter which had to be resolved was the question of the admissibility in evidence of the 'confession' allegedly made by the boy. The defence objected to this being tendered in evidence on the basis that in all the circumstances such a confession could not be said to be voluntary and accordingly a 'trial', in the absence of the jury, was held to decide this issue. The police officer gave evidence that, so far as he was concerned, the boy appeared to be making the confession of his own free will and he did not put any pressure upon him at all. He denied 'assisting' him in any way as to what the confession should contain. He did, however, admit that the boy had not made any admission of guilt throughout the whole period he had been in the cell in the police station until he made his confession, and that for the majority of that period he had been naked in a cell apart from his underpants and a blanket. The defence were in possession of a statement made by the social worker who had been present at the time when the confession was made. In this statement the social worker had made it quite clear that what was involved was far from a 'voluntary' confession that had been freely made. Whatever had been said was as the result of an interrogation with leading questions being regularly fired by the officer. The social worker was called by the defence as a witness. He failed to give the essential evidence which he had earlier given in his statement to the defence lawyers and which he had signed. (The reader ought to be made aware that if a witness called on behalf of either of the parties at a trial gives evidence which is merely inconsistent with what he alleged in an earlier statement he cannot be cross examined by the party who called him by putting to him his earlier statement. He merely becomes what is known in law as an unfavourable witness. Accordingly the social worker could not be cross examined on the basis of his earlier statement.) A psychiatrist then gave evidence of the fact that the boy was backward for his years. The judge ruled that the 'confession' was voluntary and admissible in evidence. Defence counsel informed counsel for the Crown that he did not intend to call the social worker at the trial and accordingly released him to the Crown in the hope that they would call him as a witness. (Had they done so he could then have been cross examined by the defence on the basis of his previous statement.)

Another issue had to be resolved before the trial could commence. The coloured boy who had previously pleaded guilty to the offences was prepared to give evidence for the defence of the fact that he had given the boy the pills and a quantity of whisky providing the judge was prepared to sentence him before he gave his evidence. If not, he feared that he would be given a greater sentence for admitting this fact. (The defence could not force him to give such evidence due to the various evidential rules concerning privilege and unfavourable witnesses.) The judge was informed of this problem but refused to sentence the coloured boy until after the trial. The coloured boy could not therefore be called with any useful purpose as a witness for the defence.

The Crown opened their case and subsequently called the various victims of the robberies. There was no evidence of identification neither was there any forensic evidence. At the close of the Crown case the only evidence against the boy consisted in the confession statement which was before the jury. The Crown had not called the social worker who had been present, and consequently the jury had not heard what was contained in the social worker's statement to the defence lawyers. It was clear, however, that the police had not wanted the boy's mother to see her son until after the 'confession' had been obtained.

The defence team were then placed in an extremely difficult position as to what advice they were to give the boy. It was clear as the reader will see very shortly that it was totally impossible for the boy to give evidence. Equally, whether or not he does give evidence must be his own decision, it is not one which can be made for him by his representatives. After listening to the various options open to him the boy decided that he would make a statement from the dock to the jury. However, this was to pose another problem of immense difficulty, for the boy could not read or write. The statement which the boy wished to make was taken down by his solicitors at his dictation and application was then made to the judge for somebody, not necessarily a member of the defence team, to read this statement to the jury, for surely a person could not be prejudiced by his own disability. The judge refused the application. The boy therefore when he made his statement to the jury was restricted to whatever he had in his mind at the time; an extremely difficult task for a competent lawyer let alone a backward boy of fifteen years of age. When making his statement he told the jury how he had been given pills and a quantity of whisky by his friend the coloured boy, how he recalled getting into the motor vehicle but could not recall anything more until he woke up in the cell. He said that what was in his alleged confession was there because the police officer had told him to say those words. He had asked to see his mother beforehand but the police had told him that they had been unable to contact her. The next witness to be called by the defence was a very eminent psychiatrist with considerable academic qualifications, who gave evidence that he had examined the boy in prison. He further gave evidence that the effect of certain pills with alcohol could produce a state of mind in which an individual would not know what he was doing in the sense of being responsible for his actions, but of course this depended on the pills which had been consumed. (What the pills were could not be proved.) He was then asked the most relevant of questions, which went something like this:

'Doctor, during your examination of the defendant were you able to form an opinion as to his mental age?'
'Yes I was.'
'What opinion did you so form?'
'In my opinion his mental age was equivalent to that of a boy of six years.'

Defence counsel sat down immediately after the answer of six years was given. Crown counsel cross examined and was only able to establish that notwithstanding his mental age he was still capable of holding a shotgun. This, however, was now hardly the issue. The judge had clearly spotted the relevance, and he then entered into a substantial cross examination of the doctor. Including in the cross examination by the judge was a question to the effect that a mental age of six might not necessarily preclude him from having a degree of cunning. Similar types of questions followed.

The boy's mother gave evidence and confirmed in effect that she had been prevented from seeing her son until after he had made his 'confession.' That was the case for the defence. Counsel for the Crown and for the defence made their closing speeches and then it was the turn of the judge to sum up the evidence.

It is now necessary for the reader to be aware that there is a cardinal principle of English law in common with the legal system of many other Western nations that, with very few exceptions, a person is only guilty of a criminal offence if at the time he commits that offence he has, simply put, a guilty mind. This principle was relevant in two circumstances so far as the present case was concerned. Firstly, assuming that the defendant did commit the acts which had been alleged against him, what was his state of mind at the time he committed them? Secondly, if he did not know what he was doing at the time when he committed those acts because for example of the combined influence of drink and drugs, then this would afford a totally separate defence, known in law as automatism.

During his summing up the judge withdrew the defence of automatism from the jury on the basis that there was no evidence to support it. (The reader will recall that the only evidence of it was what the defendant had stated in his statement to the jury from the dock. Even then he was unable to specify, perhaps not surprisingly, what pills he had taken. It is, however, difficult to understand what other evidence there could have been because in effect the judge's decision not to sentence the coloured boy until after the trial prevented the coloured boy from giving evidence.) He then went on to direct the jury that amnesia is not a defence (it had never been suggested that it was) and the vast majority of a very lengthy summing up was concerned with the prosecution case, with only one paragraph concerned with the state of mind of the defendant at the time of the commission of the offences. He pointed out to the jury that they were not bound to accept the expert evidence of the psychiatrist and that the police officer (the one who had obtained the confession) had thought he was a boy mature for his age.

The jury retired in order to consider this verdict and returned after deliberating for approximately one and a half hours to find the defendant guilty of all six offences of armed robbery.

Before the judge passed sentence he was to receive, as is customary, certain reports known as social enquiry reports, which had been prepared by totally independent people. Other reports of a similar nature were also produced. The reports made it clear that the boy was backward for his years. There was therefore overwhelming expert evidence that whatever the actual age of the boy his mental age was well below that of a boy of fifteen years. The judge passed upon him a sentence of seven years detention.

The case was to have a most interesting sequel, for an application was made to the Court of Appeal for leave to appeal against conviction. There was no justification to appeal against the sentence imposed because if he did have a guilty mind and did know what he was doing then seven years for six armed robberies could not be argued to be manifestly excessive. The main issue before the Court of Appeal was whether the judge had directed the jury properly on the law in order for them to determine whether he did have such a guilty mind.

The application first came before a single judge of the Court of Appeal who refused leave to appeal. Not deterred by this refusal, application was then made to the full court. The legal niceties of what took place are not relevant to a work of this nature with certain exceptions which are as follows: the solicitors for the defendant, who was now to be known as the appellant, and his counsel had been informed by the court beforehand that because of insufficient time the court would only deal with the application for leave and would not hear the appeal itself. The most time counsel was going to be allowed was forty-five minutes. Under those circumstances, as a full hearing of the appeal itself could well have taken all day, there was little point in counsel turning up at court with all the various authorities if there would be no time to hear them, and was content to argue the case as being a proper one fit for a full hearing by the court. Further, his instructions were merely to apply for leave to appeal and, if granted, to apply for legal aid. The court decided, notwithstanding what had earlier occurred, that they were going to deal with the matter as if they were hearing the appeal itself. Counsel, having been taken completely by surprise, informed the court of his predicament and asked for the case to be put back (heard later in the day) in order that he could prepare it fully and present the relevant authorities in support of his case. The court refused this request.

The court refused the application for leave and delivered after a short retirement a somewhat lengthy judgement. It was apparent that they had read counsel's written opinion on the matter or if not had studied his lengthy written grounds in some depth, but they were to make reference to the fact of the police officer's opinion as to the boy's mental age. It followed, therefore, that the second highest court in the land was to uphold everything the trial judge had done, and because of the approach adopted by the Court of Appeal the appellant had no right to appeal to the House of Lords.

There could be no doubt that there was ample justification for the jury's verdict if the only issue that they had been concentrating on was whether or not he had 'done it.' There was however overwhelming evidence of the boy's mental state of mind with reference to age. The starting point in the calculation was fifteen years. The only expert evidence given at the trial put it at six years. There was independent evidence after the trial that the boy was backward for his years. There was also evidence that when the gun was fired it was done so at the tin cans which had previously been neatly stacked. The question for the reader is a simple one. Assuming that the boy committed the acts are you able to say that he knew what he was doing when he committed them?

At the time of writing about this case a boy who, according to the only expert evidence given, has a mental age of six years is firmly locked up and will be so for a period of up to seven years.

Case 6

One Saturday lunchtime in the spring of 1980 a number of police officers who were on duty near a busy shopping centre arrested three young coloured boys and charged them with offences of attempted theft.

The boys were subsequently to appear before the Magistrates Court, when two of the police officers were to give the following evidence.

They stated that they had been on duty in the area looking for pickpockets as there recently had been a considerable number of complaints concerning such activity. These boys had suddenly commanded their attention and they had decided to keep observation upon them. (During cross examination they were unable to give any good reason as to why they had decided to keep observation upon these particular boys other than that they appeared suspicious.) They then saw an old lady carrying a handbag waiting in the bus queue. One of the defendants was standing immediately in front of the lady, one of the others was standing immediately behind her. As the bus approached the third defendant shoved the old lady, whereupon the one standing behind her was observed to have put his hand in her handbag before withdrawing it. (Presumably the handbag must have been opened.) They were then seen to run away to the next bus stop, which was situated approximately ten yards further down on the same side of the road, when it was alleged that their actions were repeated with another member of the public. All three were then arrested, taken to the police station and charged with attempted theft, charges which each of them strenuously denied.

The boys were then to give evidence and the evidence of the first boy was as follows: he was sixteen years of age and still at school, though he was expecting to leave school shortly. He had left home at noon on the day in question in order to go to work at a butcher's shop, a part-time job which he had had for many months. His hours of work were from 1.00pm to 5.00pm. He normally left home at about 12.15pm but on this particular day he had left about fifteen minutes earlier because he wanted to have a look at a pair of shoes which he had seen in a shop window on the way to the bus stop where he would get the bus to work. While looking in the shop window he saw two of his friends who knew that he had this Saturday job and who asked him whether he would take them along with him to see whether they had any other vacancies. (There was independent corroboration of the fact of the boy's employment at the butchers.) This he agreed to do. He then explained that there were a number of buses which he could get (this was also independently corroborated) and seeing one approaching all three of them joined the bus queue. As the bus arrived there was some pushing in the queue and the bus looked fairly full. Then they noticed another bus a short distance behind. As the bus got nearer to him he was able to see its number and knew that this bus stopped at the other bus stop some ten yards further along. They then ran from the queue in which they were standing and joined the queue at the next bus stop, whereupon they were arrested. He totally denied the police allegations. His two friends gave similar evidence corroborating his story. None of their evidence was shaken by cross examination from the prosecution.

The magistrates dismissed the case against them and then took the most unusual step of awarding the defendant's legal costs against the police on the basis that in their view this was a case which ought not to have been brought.

As a result of failing to turn up for work on that particular Saturday the boy had lost his part-time job.

As he came out of the court room he appeared somewhat aggrieved and said the following words to his counsel:

'Thanks guv. you did a great job. But what about all my mates who can't get jobs because they have previous convictions for offences which they didn't commit. They were not so lucky.'

The writer had intended to finish these examples of specific case histories with a case of rape. The problem was which specific case of rape to choose, but recent publicity on the topic has prompted me to deal with this example in general terms, and then to refer to a specific case history.

Rape is a very serious offence punishable upon conviction with a maximum sentence of life imprisonment. Rarely, if ever, can there be justification for a sentence other than an immediate custodial one. Many people in very high positions of authority have been quick to criticise a recent sentence imposed by a judge on a man who had been convicted of rape and which amounted to a fine. Equally there has been very strong criticism from the same or similar people at the way the police investigate complaints of rape, in particular their handling of the victim. I use the word 'victim' because many of those who criticised have used the word. As far as the writer is aware not one of these people who have been so ready to raise public disquiet about these matters has been prepared in the same context of their criticism to put the other side of the coin, or if they have it hasn't been reported. This other side is often far more tragic than can possibly be imagined.

To begin with a woman is not a victim of rape but a complainant. She becomes a victim after the case has been proved against the rapist or he has pleaded guilty to the charge. There are numerous allegations of rape brought each year and a substantial proportion of the men who are charged are acquitted. In many of these cases where a verdict of not guilty has been returned there are a substantial number of women members who make up the jury.

Allegations of rape tend to fall into two main categories. Firstly, when the allegation is made by a woman against a man she has previously known or had a connection with. Secondly, when the allegation is made against a stranger. In all cases, whatever the woman's previous sexual experiences (for example she may be a full time prostitute who has brought many similar allegations) details of such matters can never be brought out at the trial without leave of the court.

No other criminal offence regularly causes as much havoc to the lives of an innocent defendant than this one. From the moment the decision is taken to commence proceedings the defendant will often have difficulty in obtaining bail because of the serious nature of the charge. He will often lose his job and even when he has been acquitted many months later his family life, if not totally destroyed, will never be the same again. No action is ever taken against women who, as a result of malice, spite or other doubtful motives, are able to bring the full force of the legal system down upon the heads of innocent victims. Even when the innocent man is eventually acquitted such women have, to a large extent, achieved their object. The numbers of innocent men who have been stretched to the very lengths of human misery and degradation as a result of such false allegations are substantial. The ease with which such a situation can occur is abhorrent. While it is clearly right that those who are guilty of such an offence should be severely punished, it is positively shameful that those occupying positions of power have totally failed to put the other side of the story when an innocent man is wrongly accused.

The efficient and responsible police officer has, for a long time, been aware of the turmoil which a false allegation can cause. It is for this reason that when he interviews a complaint of rape he does not wear kid gloves. True, it means that the person who makes the genuine complaint is then often subjected to an embarrassing ordeal (it matters not whether she is interviewed by a male or female police officer because if the allegation is to be denied she may have to go through a much more testing ordeal by way of cross examination at the time of the trial), but this can never be as bad as the alleged crime itself. It is soon over, and it gives the police officer the opportunity of sifting out the malicious or unfounded allegation and thus saving an innocent man from the total destruction of his personal life.

Now as a result of the undoubted pressure which has been put upon the police force in respect of such charges, many more proceedings for rape will be brought based on little evidence. Many more innocent men will be eventually acquitted only to find their lives totally destroyed. One can only hope that before there are further public outbursts upon this highly sensitive subject account will be taken of the views of the wives of innocent men who have been accused of rape, and the effect which such an allegation has had upon their own lives.

Case 7

The prosecution case was as follows:
Mrs Williams, a highly respectable lady in her late thirties,

owned a restaurant in the centre of a large city. On the first floor above the restaurant was a tastefully furnished two bedroomed flat which she occupied as her home and had lived there alone for approximately the past twelve months since she divorced her husband.

One evening in April Mrs Williams closed the restaurant at approximately midnight after the last guest had left and the staff had finished clearing up and in accordance with her normal practice took the till drawer upstairs with her. She fell asleep by approximately 1.00am but unbeknown to her she was shortly to embark on one of the most terrifying experiences of her lifetime.

At 4.30am wearing only her nightdress in bed she was awoken to find a young man in his early twenties (who she alleged was the defendant) with a carving knife at her throat. He was shabbily dressed, his face was dirty, his hair was filthy and his hands were full of grease, so much so that when he was later to force one of his hands into her mouth she could taste the grease, which to her seemed like the grease one finds in connection with motor vehicles.

He dug his fingernails into the inside of her thighs, forcing her legs apart, undid his trousers and forced his penis into her vagina. As intercourse was taking place he was groping at her body and viciously biting her left breast just above the nipple.

After he had finished he forced her out of the bed and at knifepoint made her show him where the money was. He was not however even satisfied with this, taking approximately £3,000 worth of jewellery with him and then pushing her back against the base of the bed with such force that she suffered substantial brusing. He then made his escape leaving Mrs Williams in a distressed condition.

Soon after the attack Mrs Williams put on a clean pair of knickers and went to summon help. The police were very quickly on the scene and a fingerprint of the defendant's was found downstairs in the restaurant. Mrs Williams was then examined by a woman police doctor who found bruising to the face and body. The vulva was red and the vagina appeared sore. The police doctor was also to testify to the distressed state of the victim. Semen was found inside the vagina and in the crutch of her knickers this semen was found to be of blood group 'A', the same blood group as the defendant.

Approximately eight months later Mrs Williams recalled where she had seen her alleged attacker before. He had been in the restaurant earlier that evening with a group of people all of whom were particularly scruffy looking. By then the defendant was in custody for another and unrelated matter. Mrs Williams attended an identification parade and without any hesitation identified the defendant as being the man who raped and robbed her.

The defendant was interviewed at length by the police. He was a man of bad character with numerous previous convictions for burglary and theft, none for any sexual offence or for any offence of violence against the person prior to the alleged offences against Mrs Williams. During his interview by the police he admitted going to the restaurant that evening with friends after having been working on a friend's car, admitted having motor vehicle grease or oil on his hands and/or clothing, and admitted going back to the restaurant after it had closed for the purpose of stealing money which he needed to get married. (He had subsequently got married to a woman of good character.)

He admitted breaking into the restaurant through the glass in the back door and taking the money from the till which according to him was approximately £150, whereupon he heard a noise upstairs and ran. On making his escape into the street he turned around to see a man who was swearing at him. He denied raping Mrs Williams, using a knife and denied ever going upstairs to her private flat. He alleged that the time when he burgled the restaurant was approximately 1.00am.

The reader will be immediately aware that the proposition that Mrs Williams was being raped and robbed by somebody else when the defendant happened to be burgling the restaurant, while remotely possible is so highly improbable as to be absurd.

After a period of nearly two years had elapsed since the alleged incident the defendant was to stand his trial in the most famous courtroom in the world, court 1 at the Old Bailey. Following the concern uttered by various sections of society, Parliament and even the Prime Minister in connection with the quality of judges who should try rape cases, one of the most senior and experienced High Court Judges was to try the case. The jury were empanelled and defence counsel challenged two very young girls who had been called to sit on the jury. He did so not because of their sex but because of their age, for he would have been quite happy to have had an all female jury providing they were at least in their mid-twenties and on-wards, and consequently would have been more likely to have had a greater experience of life than a young girl of approximately twenty-one years of age. The jury finally empanelled consisted of nine men and three women with an average age of approximately thirty-five.

The learned judge right throughout the trial was making quite clear, albeit by inference, what his personal view was, namely that the defendant was guilty, and at one stage during the cross examination of the victim (after all why should the victim of such an alleged monstrous attack have to go through this further ordeal of public cross examination) clashed with defence counsel accusing him of not doing his job properly! His summing up to the jury left nobody in any doubt whom he believed, including such language as:

'you should think very carefully indeed before you reject the evidence of this woman of impeccable character, in favour of the evidence of the defendant.'

The jury took nearly five hours to reach their verdicts, which were unanimous and were as follows:

Count one, the offence of rape – not guilty.
Count two, the offence of robbery – not guilty.
Count three, the offence of burglary – guilty but not of the jewellery.

Had the verdicts been left to the police, the prosecuting counsel and the learned judge it must be fair comment to say that there would have been the most monstrous injustice caused in this case. In order to obtain some insight into how the jury reached those verdicts the defence case has to be looked at in greater detail, for although it is not possible to know exactly what went on in the jury room, unless one was present at the time, this was one of those rare cases where the only reasonable justification for the jury's verdicts was that they had accepted the defence case. This was most unlikely to have been a situation of the jury merely not being sure of guilt.

The defence had adopted the view that there were only three possibilities. Firstly, Mrs Williams was telling the truth but was mistaken about the identity of her attacker. This view was instantly discarded for the reasons given above, for it is absurd to suggest that Mrs Williams was being raped by an intruder after or at the same time as she was being burgled by the defendant. Secondly, Mrs Williams was telling the truth but the defendant was lying. Thirdly, Mrs Williams was lying and the defendant was telling the truth.

The following evidence was elicited during the trial.

(a) No fingerprints which could be identified as belonging to the defendant were found in the first floor of the premises.

(b) No identifiable fingerprints of anybody were found on the till drawer, which itself was found in the first floor of the premises near the bed.

(c) Mrs Williams had been paid out by the insurance company many months prior to her making her statement as to remembering when she had seen the defendant prior to the alleged attack.

(d) A fragment of glass was found underneath Mrs Williams' fingernails along with traces of grease and oil.

(e) No identifiable fingerprints were found around the point of forced entry into the premises.

(f) Numerous inconsistencies were apparent between the statement which Mrs Williams had given to the police shortly after the alleged attack and her evidence in court. In particular in her statement to the police she had stated that she had telephoned for help whereas when giving evidence from the witness box she said that she physically left the premises to get help.

(g) Mrs Williams had maintained right up until she gave evidence that her alleged attacker had not ejaculated, and she also attributed to him a statement which he had allegedly made during the act of intercourse. If it had been made this statement corroborated the fact of non-ejaculation, but when giving evidence she said that she believed he had ejaculated.

There were certain other factors which troubled defence counsel. If the defendant was lying why lie about the time of the burglary? The defendant's girlfriend, who was later to become his wife, was a slim attractive girl in her very early twenties and of good character. She was to give evidence that she rarely refused the defendant sexual intercourse and he was never violent. The defendant, although he had been in trouble before had, until then, never been convicted of an offence involving any form of violence to the person.

Assuming the defendant was telling the truth there was only one sequence of events which fitted all the material facts and fitted them like a glove. The defendant had been downstairs stealing the money from the till drawer which was at that time in the till and which was downstairs in the restaurant. He was then disturbed by a man who was upstairs and who in all probability recognised him. Whether this man was or was not having sexual intercourse with Mrs Williams at the time and if so whether such intercourse had got out of hand is something which only he and Mrs Williams know, but he was there not as a trespasser but by invitation. After the defendant had left a cunning scheme was embarked upon, with one object, namely to defraud the insurance company. The till drawer was taken upstairs and at some stage wiped clean of all fingerprints and the point where forced entry into the premises had been made was also wiped clean of fingerprints. The police were then summoned and the allegation of rape was made. The insurance company would have been less likely to have made any thorough investigation or had their suspicions aroused if they thought that their 'client' had also been raped. As long as the burglar (the defendant) was not caught Mrs Williams was safe from exposure and even if he was caught she always had the rape to fall back on, for who would believe the word of a burglar as opposed to hers. She knew that there was very little likelihood of the burglar being caught in the absence of fingerprints and in the light of her failure to tell the police where she had seen him before. However, many

months later he was arrested in connection with a totally
different matter, and the police had not forgotten about the
'rape'. Mrs Williams was then summoned to an identification
parade, when panic obviously set in, for as a philosopher once
said, 'what a tangled web we weave when we endeavour to
deceive'. The fact that the motive for her telling lies was the
insurance fraud was clearly put to Mrs Williams by defence
counsel. She denied it.

The sad part about the whole affair is that the learned judge
could not see it and even when the jury returned their verdicts
he was still to sentence the defendant to twelve months immediate imprisonment for the burglary which he had always
admitted. A man who had never been in prison before, who
now appeared to have settled down with an attractive wife
who by then was six months pregnant, who had nothing else
hanging over his head and who had such serious charges
hanging over his head for such a length of time was going to
swell the ranks of the prison population at substantial public
expense.

Regrettably it must by now be apparent to the reader that
injustice can readily be the rule as opposed to the exception.
To provide details of numerous other cases would add little to
what has already been illustrated. Comment upon injustice
within the civil law when due to the fact that a defendant is
denied a jury would equally add little. The fact that such
injustice is rampant must be accepted by those in power before
remedial measures can ever be effective.

GENERAL OBSERVATIONS AND REMEDIES

Any code of human rights must of necessity, whatever its individual provisions, assume the proposition that an individual accused of a criminal offence will always receive a fair trial and that an innocent person will never have to spend one day in prison unless it is absolutely necessary. The various theories behind much which takes place within the criminal law branch of the English legal system along with the laws themselves are undoubtedly consistent with basic human rights, principles of fair play and natural instincts of justice. When, however, the various theories coupled with the laws themselves are put into practice, what actually takes place is often something entirely different, and there is overwhelming evidence, as has been clearly demonstrated throughout this book, that the criminal law branch of the legal system does not live up to the standards expected by ordinary law abiding citizens. Further, the operation of the criminal law offends many of the fundamental concepts of human rights.

The time for moderation of language is over. The ordinary law abiding and hard working people who, together, form one of the finest nations in the world are undeserving of having had thrust upon them the legal system which actually exists and which is so obviously rampant in perversity. No individual part can be picked out in isolation as being the effective cause for the present situation, for each is equally faulty, and just like a number of individual cells, each diseased with their own cancerous growth, will combine together to produce eventual destruction, so the various arms of the legal system appear to have combined to make a mockery of justice and liberty.

There is no point in highlighting the number of prisoners in overcrowded prisons without first asking how many of them are innocent and yet to be tried. Neither is there any point in putting civil disturbance automatically down to unemployment without first asking how many of those who have taken part have been denied employment because of previous convictions for offences of which they were not guilty, or how many have a justifiable sense of grievance as a result of being unfairly treated by the legal system.

People who because of their criminal activities are a danger to other law abiding members of society must of necessity be deprived of their liberty, but a failure effectively to differentiate between the innocent and the guilty is a failure to recognise the ineptitude and inefficiency of the system itself.

The doctrine of collectivism, justified in certain times of war or matters involving national security, must never be allowed to defeat or undermine the doctrine of freedom of speech. The good, conscientious police officer ought never to find himself branded as a result of the unscrupulous dishonest officer. The judge who has built up a reputation based upon fairness coupled with the ability to dispense justice in a proper manner ought never to find his reputation and ability prejudiced because of any of his inefficent, less competent or less worthy colleagues. The 'old boy network' which often predominates within the professions must be buried forever, leaving merit to become the predominant factor, and 'character' to be given its ordinary meaning as understood by the ordinary law abiding citizen. People in the various positions of power and authority within the legal system who are unable to live up to the standards of merit expected of them by a free society ought never to be able to shelter behind the skirts of what is rapidly becoming an abominable doctrine due to its use in situations for which is is totally unsuited.

To carry on in the present arbitrary manner. is to heap injustice upon injustice, to deny liberty and remove freedom, to compound iniquity within the system until the good which does exist becomes so deeply immersed as to be invisible to all but the very few. When such a situation arises then people begin to look for alternative political remedies in order to solve the problem. This can easily lead to the extremities of political theories, and whatever freedom we have at present may then be lost forever.

The remedies are not easy, but first there must be an acceptance of the inadequacies which do in fact exist. It is useless attempting to justify them or to deny their existence, and being over-sensitive to attacks from all those who dare to criticise. An acceptance must be coupled with the will to at least try to achieve a remedy as opposed to merely pointing to other legal systems on the grounds that they are equally bad or worse.

The writer is unable to provide the reader with all the remedies, for it has been a difficult enough task to diagnose the disease and to establish some of its causes without formulating a cure, but there is one remedy which is obvious and which shines through with clarity. This is a remedy which will protect the people from abuses by those in positions of power and which successive Governments of different political allegiances have been so reticent in providing. It is a remedy which has been firmly established for many years in the United States of America: a written constitution for the people. Such a document must never be enacted by Parliament adopting its normal legislative function, for whatever its provisions if it were enacted in this manner it could easily be repealed by another Parliament. To prevent such a situation arising the content of a constitution must be declared by the highest court in the land and declared on the basis that such law is constitutional law properly so called and can never be repealed by Statute law but only by the people themselves. The detailed contents of such a constitution must be determined after consultation with Parliament and all interested parties, and most important of all with the people themselves. While its content will be a question of debate, if it were to be derived on the basis that such constitutional law, in theory, already exists, though not in writing, and if its principles were to be derived from basic principles of equity, then it must surely form a solid protection for the individual against unwarranted attacks by the State.

A genuine endeavour to decide upon and to put into effect

the contents of a written constitution could easily lead to far greater rewards than are at a first glance imaginable. Begin by considering a code which is readily acceptable to the overwhelming majority of ordinary people. Such a code would be taught in our schools to our children with the consequence that within, perhaps, the space of one or two generations an overwhelming mass of the population would be of one mind in respect of certain fundamental issues contained in such a code. Consider also if the same code were to be adopted and implemented not merely by one nation but by all nations; then, in the same way, would not all the nations be of one mind concerning the basic principles of justice contained within the code? If such a situation were to occur what could easily be the result? The answer is relatively simple. The threat to world peace is world wars. Wars are started for a variety of different reasons but they all have one thing in common, namely that at least two or more groups of people differ upon certain fundamental principles which each group considers as essential for its own survival. These principles can often be traced to differing interpretations of the basic concept of justice. A common understanding and acceptance of these basic concepts with acquiescence by all must of necessity lead along the only true path to world peace.